Handel's Messiah
and His English
Oratorios

T0347887

MAGNUM OPUS
Edited by Robert Levine

Magnum Opus is a series for anyone seeking a greater
familiarity with the cornerstones of Western Classical
Music—operatic, choral, and symphonic. An erudite collection
of passionate, down-to-earth, and authoritative books on the
works and their creators, Magnum Opus will build into an
indispensable resource for anyone's musical library.

Also Available:
Beethoven's Fifth and Seventh Symphonies by David Hurwitz
Brahms' Symphonies by David Hurwitz

Handel's Messiah and His English Oratorios

A CLOSER LOOK

Ben Finane

continuum

NEW YORK • LONDON

2009

The Continuum International Publishing Group Inc
80 Maiden Lane, New York, NY 10038

The Continuum International Publishing Group Ltd
The Tower Building, 11 York Road, London SE1 7NX
www.continuumbooks.com

Library of Congress Cataloging-in-Publication Data
Finane, Ben.
Handel's Messiah and his English oratorios : a closer look / Ben Finane.
    p. cm. – (Magnum opus)
Includes bibliographical references.
ISBN-13: 978-0-8264-2943-8 pbk.
ISBN-10: 0-8264-2943-2 pbk.
1. Handel, George Frideric, 1685-1759. Messiah. 2. Handel, George
Frideric, 1685-1759. Oratorios. 3. Oratorio–18th century.
I. Title. II. Series.

ML410.H13F37 2009
782.23092–dc22   2009013701

Contents

Acknowledgments

Thanks to Robert Levine for his trust, wisdom, and patience.

Thanks too to teachers and mentors past and present for guidance on music, writing, and writing on music: Bradley Bambarger, Susan Benston, Curt Cacioppo, Menon Dwarka, Richard Freedman, Marc Puricelli, Debora Sherman, and Matthew Westphal. A collective thank-you to the music faculty of the 92nd Street Y, who raised my game a notch during an administrative tenure there. Thanks to sharp readers Ashley Opalka and Monika Stump. Special thanks to Maria Kakoulides for spiritual insight.

Introduction

MUCH HAS BEEN MADE OF the fact that Handel wrote *Messiah*, the most popular work in all of choral literature, in the space of 24 days. But Handel had been preparing to write this work all his life. *Messiah* is Handel's perfect storm. It was composed as an English oratorio, a genre Handel invented out of necessity to meet the conditions of his market, one that served a sacred-music audience while maximizing his talents in operatic, instrumental and choral writing. But *Messiah* is unique among Handel's oratorios in that its ethereal narrative freed him from the usual operatic temptations and distractions of plot, action, and character and forced the composer into a meditative corner, where he created a masterpiece that takes on nothing less than Death, Resurrection and Redemption. Handel did so in resplendent fashion and yet—and this is more astounding—he did so modestly and accessibly.

Upon first opening the score to *Messiah*, I was not struck by an arresting and overwhelming genius that leapt from the page, but rather met with a simplicity of design so humble and unassuming that I had to check the spine to be assured that I wasn't looking at an orchestral reduction. But no, that's really all there was to it. Flipping through the score, the staves continued to fit comfortably on the page, two or three at a time. Voice parts, *basso continuo*, and violins; often with cello and viola; often without any strings apart from *continuo*; occasionally with trumpet, oboe, and timpani. That was it. He wrote all that with this? I reasoned that there must then be some complex harmonic changes, shifts in key, distant modulations. I took a deep breath, turned up the sensitivity of my music-theory radar, gave the score another pass, and found nothing. Everything was clear and revealed itself after modest examination. Meter? Standard. Tricky rhythms? Clever moves that were well placed, but nothing deceptive. What then is the secret to the genius and unshakable integrity of *Messiah*? I believe the answer lies somewhere in the dictated modesty of the composition itself, which does not reach up to God through majestic gesture but rather seeks Him earthbound through humility and subjugation of the ego. *Messiah* does not employ empty flourish or ornamentation; its coloration serves an aim greater than itself: the realization of a pristine libretto that strives to encapsulate the basic message of Christian Redemption. In chiseling out this message, Handel finds a kinship with twentieth-century writer Antoine de Saint-Exupery, who asserted that perfection is achieved not when there is nothing more to add, but when there is nothing left to take away. If meager in its texture, the richness of *Messiah* is undeniable and worthy of investigation.

Chapter 1

Handel: A Brief Biography

OFTEN REFERRED TO AS AN ENGLISH COMPOSER, George Frideric Handel (1685–1759) was in fact a German chameleon, a man who, over the course of his life, worked under the patronage of cardinals in Rome, princes in Germany, and Queen Anne and King George of Great Britain. One of the greatest composers of his era and an opportunist in the best sense, Handel contributed to every musical genre of the time and invented a new one—namely the English oratorio, the genre to which his most celebrated work, *Messiah,* belongs. He was, by various accounts, jovial, gluttonous, impetuous, risible, and irascible, and, by all accounts, good-hearted, honest, fervent, and charitable.

Handel[1] was born Georg Friederich Händel in Halle an der Saale, in the German state of Saxony, the son of Georg Händel, a surgeon and barber, and Dorothea Taust, daughter of a pastor and second wife to Händel senior. The house in which he grew up was located in Giebichenstein, a suburb

---

1 Handel dropped his umlaut after moving to England.

3

of Halle, and the dwelling was known as *Zum gelben Hirsch*, "At the Yellow Stag," a former tavern. Through political maneuvering, Handel's father was able to keep the liquor license attached to the lot, and made some money on the side selling wine.

The earliest music education for Handel came at the age of seven under Friedrich Zachow, organist at the Liebfrauen-kirche at Halle. Under Zachow's tutelage, the young man learned composition and how to play organ, harpsichord and violin, while becoming familiar with a variety of national styles and a large collection of Italian and German music. His studies with Zachow were likely the foundation of what would become Handel's impressive musical adaptability (all the more formidable when paired with his social ease), while his training in pastiche doubtless encouraged later tendencies to "borrow" rather generously from other composers.

Though many composers have historically borrowed from their own output (Handel certainly) and have been heavily influenced by their mentors and predecessors, Handel's practice of lifting wholesale the music of others for inclusion in his own was largely unique. Articles on Handel's plagiarism surfaced as early as 1722 when the composer Johann Mattheson showed that Handel had taken one of Mattheson's arias note-for-note for his opera *Agrippina*. Charles Jennens, Handel's librettist for *Messiah*, wrote in a letter in 1743 of his trepidation over lending Handel Italian opera scores, writing, "I dare say I shall catch him stealing from them." Handel's "borrowing" practices were more fully documented in a magazine article in 1822 and then through the nineteenth and twentieth centuries. Suffice it to say that Handel borrowed from everyone and throughout his career.

Taken in the context of Handel's aesthetic and worldview, however, we can view this practice not as laziness or thievery, but rather, from Handel's perspective, as an extension of his avant-garde worldview of musical parity and as recognition of the equality of musical material and ideas—from any source. Ultimately, Handel's borrowing benefits his music and his listeners alike.

His father was adamant that Handel become a lawyer, but his death left Handel at the age of 12 free to pursue his musical studies without further worry of fatherly resistance. In 1702, Handel enrolled in the University of Halle, showing evidence that a liberal-arts education was not neglected, at least initially. But Handel, raised in the Lutheran conformity, soon received an appointment as organist at the Calivinist Domkirche and began devoting himself entirely to music.

Feeling Halle too small for his talents, in 1703 Handel moved to Hamburg, giving him access to a city that had the distinction of hosting Germany's sole opera company operating outside the courts. This would enormously aid his musical growth. Under the aegis of Hamburg opera manager-composer Reinhard Keiser, Handel went from a third-desk violinist to harpsichordist-conductor. Absorbing Keiser's music as his own, Handel also gleaned from the composer the aesthetic of a mix of national styles: French, German, and Italian. In his operas, Keiser would mix Italian aria with German recitative and French librettos that could be stretched as needed to accommodate any manner of side-plots and subterfuge. This mix of styles was common to music of the Baroque period (1600–1750). (The word "baroque" derives from the Portuguese word meaning "irregular pearl," which is an apt, if latent characterization of both the architecture and the music of the period.) An examination of the Baroque suite, a collection of short instrumental pieces often written for keyboard, reveals a juxtaposition of various dance forms from throughout Europe. Movements might include the Allemande ("German" in French(!)), a dance at a moderate tempo with origins in the Renaissance; the Gigue, a dance in compound form from the English jig; and the Passepied, a fast dance found in later suites by Bach and Handel. While the Italian opera style became cemented in Handel's music during his travels to Italy a bit later in his life, he never abandoned the French and German elements.

In Hamburg Handel made the acquaintance of the composer Johann Mattheson (1681–1764), whose *Grundlage einer Ehren-Pforte* (*An Opening Gateway*), a lexicon detailing biographical information on over a hundred composers, provides much insight to Handel's early musical growth. The book also details an early life-threatening drama for Handel, in which he fought a duel with the author following a performance of Mattheson's *Cleopatra*. Mattheson not only wrote the opera, but also sang the role of Antonius (who commits suicide a half hour before the end of the opera). Mattheson had been accustomed to, once dead, going into to the orchestra pit and accompanying the rest of the opera from the harpsichord. Handel, however, refused to give up his seat at the instrument, so the two fought a duel (not uncommon practice at the time) at the exit of the Opera House in front of a crowd of onlookers. Fortunately for Handel, Mattheson shattered his blade on one of Handel's brass buttons, and the two were soon reconciled.

Opportunity arose for Handel to compose his first opera, *Almira*, as a result of Keiser's departure from Hamburg for

Brunswick and Weissenfels during the 1704–1705 season of the Hamburg opera house. *Almira* showed a penchant for the more Italian operatic style championed by Keiser as opposed to the French style of Mattheson, but its success may have stemmed from the way it happily married Italian, French, and German elements together. Some of the more ornate aspects of the work (especially its subterfuge-ridden plot) reflect the French influence, as does the use of the French Overture, which features a slow stately opening followed by a section of livelier music. The German libretto, by Friedrich Christian Feustking, was translated and adapted from an Italian libretto for the same work.

Handel's penchant for the Italian aesthetic and fluency in the style of the high Italian aria attracted the interest of Gian Gastone de Medici, the Prince of Tuscany, who encountered Handel's music while on a cultural visit to Hamburg. Invited to Italy by the Prince, Handel spent time from 1706–1710 in Florence, Naples, Rome, and Venice. It was in Italy that his musical style, heretofore a sort of international gumbo, coalesced. In Italy, he attained a greater fluency in church music and cantatas, notably with *Dixit Dominus* (1707), which shows strength in choral textures, imitation, and counterpoint. In the same year Handel wrote his first oratorio *Il trionfo del Tempo e del Disinganno*, which demonstrates significant advancement since *Almira* for his aria fluency and libretto management as well as the overall balance of the work. Ever the international, Handel, during his Italian years (a Lutheran under Catholic cardinals), was known as Giorgio Federico Hendel.

Handel had many patrons in Rome, including Cardinals Ottoboni, Pamphili, and Marquis Ruspoli. During his

Roman residency, there was a papal ban on opera, but the composer set psalms and found an outlet for operatic forms in the Italian secular cantata. His first Italian opera, *Rodrigo*, likely premiered by Ferdinando di Medici, was presented in Florence. Under Pamphili, Handel wrote the cantata *Il delirio amoroso*, which evokes the madness of a journey through the realm of the dead, as well as *Il trionfo del Tempo*, an oratorio that follows the heroine's (La Bellezza) ultimate embrace of enlightened values, thanks to the sobering advice of Il Disinganno. Venice saw the premiere of *Agrippina*, Handel's second Italian opera, a satire-comedy. The opera met with great success, demonstrating a greater assurance in form and craft than Handel had displayed in *Rodrigo*. Buoyed by its faster pacing, the psychological probing of the characters, and enhanced by the pristine quality of its arias, *Agrippina* is considered Handel's first true operatic masterpiece.

Following the conclusion of *Agrippina*'s run in 1710, Handel made his way to Germany, where he was appointed Kapellmeister to Georg Ludwig, the Elector of Hanover. There he earned 20 times his salary at the Domkirche in Halle and thrilled the court with his exceptional harpsichord playing. The Hanover period included the composition of a fine dramatic cantata, *Apollo e Dafne*, which depicts the Greek god Apollo's tragic obsession with an indifferent nymph and features a bright instrumentation that includes flute, oboe, and bassoon in addition to the usual strings.

Handel took a leave of absence almost immediately after securing the Hanover post in order to visit London, where Italian opera (sung by Italian singers) had been introduced in 1705 and was winning the battle against the budding genre of English opera. It is important to note that the London opera scene at this time was a burgeoning and bustling one, with opera houses in direct competition and opera itself serving as the nightly choice of entertainment for many, rather than being relegated to special occasions. The now-called George Frideric Handel sought out the Italian opera company at the Queen's Theatre in the Haymarket. His music had preceded him, so the marriage between Handel and London was natural, with Handel's need for an operatic venue matched by the Haymarket all-Italian company's need for an opera composer. Handel's first London opera, *Rinaldo*, was also the first commissioned by the Haymarket company and was premiered in February 1711. *Rinaldo* was well received for its tuneful music (some of which was reworked from his earlier Italian operas) and for its spectacular staging, which included a number of onstage "supers" to represent the armies and its remarkable scenery, including a mountain in Act III that rose to the ceiling of the theatre and live birds who were to fly among the onstage trees—to say nothing of the thunder, lightning, and fireworks. During the run of 15 performances, Handel was also able to display his brilliance on harpsichord to full effect.

He made a brief return to Hanover in 1711 before obtaining leave of the Elector for a second visit to England, on condition that he promised to return within a reasonable time. This was a promise he failed to keep, which would lead to his amicable dismissal from Hanover service in 1713. Handel eventually found himself inexorably tied to Georg Ludwig, however, when the Elector became King George I in 1714.

Back in London, Handel was introduced to the Earl of Burlington, under whose patronage he remained from 1713 to 1716. A follow-up to *Rinaldo*, the courtly, pastoral

Il pastor fido was unsuccessful. Noted one diarist: "[T]he scene represented only the Country of Arcadia; the Habits [costumes] were old—the Opera short."[2] Handel returned to form with grand characters and dazzling effects in *Teseo*— along with a revival of *Rinaldo*—in 1713. It was also during this period that he was asked to compose music to serve as escort for King George I on his trip up the River Thames; the orchestral suite *Water Music* was the result, and the work and its spectacular presentation added greatly to Handel's fame. The project demonstrated Handel's loyalty to the king and galvanized the relationship, and, as another testament to Handel's business savvy, perhaps also helped to secure six months' salary in arrears from Hanover.

With the help of commissions from King George I, Handel continued to write choral music and also composed Italian cantatas and music for keyboard. He published an authorized collection of the latter in 1720, *Suites de pièces*, largely driven by a previously published pirated collection. In the preface to the collection, Handel noted that he was "obliged to publish Some of the following lessons because Surreptitious and incorrect copies of them had got abroad" making it plain that his concern was providing access to integral versions of his keyboard music rather than lost profits.

With the pressures of the Jacobite rebellion in 1715 and accumulating managerial and financial concerns, the Haymarket Opera Company closed in the fall of 1717. Handel, however, managed to secure private patronage from James Brydges, Earl of Carnarvon, later the Duke of Chandos. Brydges was based in Cannons, north London.

---

2 Hicks, "Pastor fido, Il," Grove Music Online ed. L. Macy (Accessed 2008). http://www.grovemusic.com

While there, Handel composed *Acis and Galatea*, an English masque with a libretto based on Dryden's translation of Ovid's *Metamorphoses*; the first English oratorio, *Esther*, which relates the Old Testament story of Queen Esther and her victory over the anti-Semitic minister, Haman; and 11 anthems that would come to be known as the "Chandos" anthems. Later revivals of *Esther* and *Acis and Galatea* led to a series of English oratorios, the genre that would make Handel's lasting reputation.

A large part of Handel's life for the next decade was spent in service to The Royal Academy of Music, which was created in London by a group of noblemen to help ensure that Italian opera retained a place in English society. Many of the founders were also amateur musicians. While the Academy was set up with the goal of turning a profit, with "Undertakers" seeking gains of "at least five and twenty percent upon twenty percent of the Stock," these ambitions were soon understood by its directors and their "subscribers" to be unlikely, and so financial aspirations shifted to opera for opera's sake and artistic patronage. The king incorporated the Academy in 1719 and gave it a £1,000 annual budget, which gave it the form of a joint-stock corporation, a rather prescient set-up when compared to today's performing-arts venues and companies.

Handel was sent by the Lord Chamberlain to enlist singers from Europe for purposes of singing in the Academy's company, with particular pressure to enlist the great Italian castrato, Francesco Bernardi, a.k.a. Senesino (Italian for "one from Siena"), renowned for his coloratura. Successful in his mission, Handel was appointed Master of the Orchestra. The relationship between Senesino and Handel was long, rich, and tempestuous. Immediately engaged as *primo uomo* (lead male singer) at the Academy, Senesino's first Handel production was a 1720 revival of *Radamisto*, an opera about dynastic warfare in Asia Minor. Senesino would remain largely in London over the course of the next 16 years, integrating himself into high society. He would go on to create 17 lead roles for Handel, including Giulio Cesare, Orlando, and Bertarido in *Rodelinda*. Following the breakup of the Royal Academy in 1728, Senesino sang in Paris and Venice, only to reengage with Handel in 1730, singing in four more new operas and in the oratorios *Esther*, *Deborah*, and, in its bilingual version, *Acis and Galatea*. Upon leaving Handel for good to join the cross-town rival Opera of the Nobility, Senesino sang alongside the celebrated castrato Farinelli, with whom he had a famous onstage encounter in the pasticcio (Italian for "jumble" or "hodgepodge") *Artaserse*, as reported by music historian Charles Burney:

> Senesino had the part of a furious tyrant, and Farinelli that of an unfortunate hero in chains; but in the course of the first air, the captive so softened the heart of the tyrant, that Senesino, forgetting his stage-character, ran to Farinelli and embraced him in his own.

The Academy's first season (1720) opened with a production of Giovanni Porta's *Numitore*; this was followed by *Radamisto*, which was by all accounts better received than Porta's *Numitore*, an *opera seria* about the legend of Romulus and Remus now forgotten by history. The first night of *Radamisto* points to Handel's political savvy, as the composer may have delayed the opening of the opera (and shifted its position in the season's lineup) so that it coincided with the first public appearance of King George I and the Prince of Wales after their reconciliation from estrangement on St. George's day (April 23), four days before. The subject of *Radamisto*, the reuniting of a couple after a "tyrannical" love affair, doubtless helped to broker the peace between the King and Prince. The Academy had also engaged the services of the Italian composer Giovanni Bononcini (1670–1747), who opened the first full season of the Academy in November 1720 with *Astarto*, starring Senesino in the title role. Initially, Handel was overshadowed by the success of Bononcini, who was a superb composer of plaintive melodies and was noted for his text setting, particularly in recitative. Bononcini became a rival for Handel, until political events involving Jacobite conspiracies in 1722 led to a general suspicion of Catholics, which caused Bononcini to lose support among the Academy directors.

The magnificent soprano Francesca Cuzzoni arrived at the Academy in 1722, and made her debut in 1723 as Teofane, whose marriage to Otho II of Germany is the subject of Handel's *Ottone*. As Handel had not originally written the role for Cuzzoni, at the first rehearsal she initially refused to sing her opening aria, "Falsa immagine." According to Mainwairing, Handel is said to have replied: "Oh! Madame I know well that you are a real she-devil, but I hereby give you notice, me, that I am Beelzebub, the Chief of Devils." With that, Handel took Cuzzoni by the waist and swore he would throw her out the window if she said another word. Cuzzoni ironically made her reputation with the aria in question and remained a member of the company until the Royal Academy's closing in 1728, singing in every opera.

Bononcini struck back in the 1723–1724 season with two new operas (*Farnace* and *Calfurnia*), but was greatly outshone by Handel's *Giulio Cesare in Egitto*,[3] an opera filled

---

3 More frequently referred to as *Giulio Cesare*.

with soaring melodies and rich textures which also provided Senesino and Cuzzoni demanding and psychologically
probing roles as Caesar and Cleopatra. In 1723, Handel was
made Composer of Music for His Majesty's Chapel Royal, an
honorary appointment because Handel, being a foreigner,
could not hold an office of profit under the Crown. The title
recognized Handel's work in composing music for the Chapel
Royal, which included three anthems and the *Te Deum* in A.

Handel's time at the Academy cemented his Anglicization.
In 1723, he leased a house in Brook Street, London, a neigh-
borhood designed for upper- and middle-rank gentry, which
points to Handel's rising social status. It was his home
for the rest of his life. Handel served as music master to
royal princesses—Anne and Caroline, the daughters of
George II—and in 1727, became a naturalized British subject, a tangible and indisputable demonstration of his commitment to England.

The 1724–1725 season brought new Handel operas:
Tamerlano, a powerful drama about the ruler of the Tartar
Empire, and *Rodelinda*, an opera tackling a power struggle
for the throne in seventh-century Milan that ranks among
Handel's best, both musically for the wide range of emotion
expressed in its varied arias and dramatically for the por-
trayal of its sympathetic heroine. The season also enlisted
a second supreme soprano, Faustina Bordoni, who would
become a rival to Cuzzoni. For the 1725–1726 season Handel
wrote *Alessandro*, cleverly casting the two sopranos as two
princesses wooed by Alexander—which only served to fan
the flames between the divas, delighting audiences. The
next season featured a new opera, *Admeto*, again showcasing
Cuzzoni and Bordoni to great effect. The sopranos' rivalry

grew increasingly hostile and exploded in a session of onstage fisticuffs during a performance of Bononcini's *Astianatte* on June 6, 1727. It was all too much for the Princess of Wales, who was in the audience—and she abruptly closed the season. Following the brawl, the satirist John Arbuthnot published "The Devil to pay at St. James's: or A full and true Account of a most horrid and bloody Battle between Madam Faustina and Madam Cuzzoni," in which he derided the sopranos:

> Two of a Trade seldom or ever agree . . . But who would have thought the Infection should reach the Hay-market and inspire Two Singing Ladies to pull each other's Coiffs, to the no small Disquiet of the Directors, who (God help them) have enough to do to keep Peace and Quietness between them. . . . I shall not determine who is the Aggressor, but take the surer Side, and wisely pronounce them both in Fault; for it is certainly an apparent Shame that two such well bred Ladies should call Bitch and Whore, should scold and fight like any Billingsgates.

Despite (or because of) their fight, the company retained both sopranos for the 1727–1728 season in order that celebrations for the accession of the new king, George II, should go smoothly. The death of George I in June 1727 provided Handel with the occasion to write four anthems for the coronation of King George II, which included *Zadok the Priest*, a work that has been sung at every coronation of a British monarch since. The year 1727–1728 was an all-Handel season that began with *Riccardo primo* in November, taking as its subject Richard I's conquest of Cyprus; *Siroe* in February (an opera about the King of Persia); and *Tolomeo* in April, the latter being another opera designed for Cuzzoni and Faustina, who sang Seleuce and Elisa, respectively, in this opera about the banishment of Ptolemy.

At this point in the Academy's history, the financial weight of the singing roster was causing directors and subscribers to lose interest. A production of Johann Christoph Pepusch and John Gay's satiric *Beggar's Opera* (an operetta) at Lincoln's Inn Fields, a rival venue, took London by storm and remains one of the most-performed operas in English, serving as the inspiration for Bertold Brecht and Kurt Weill's *Threepenny Opera* two centuries later. *Beggar's Opera*, which took popular English ballads and Irish and French tunes already familiar to the public, managed to target the Academy with its irony, furthering the devaluation of proper opera in the eyes of the aristocracy. The resulting lack of support by many of the subscribers caused the 1728–1729 opera season to be shortened. A meeting of Academy directors in January 1729 led to the conclusion that Handel and opera house manager J. J. Heidegger should be permitted another five years of opera-making. Handel immediately left for Italy to seek out new singers for the 1729–1730 season.

Handel visited Bologna, Rome, and Venice in the spring and summer of 1729. He returned to Halle in Germany to see his mother for what would be the last time; she died in December, 1730. In Italy, he engaged a company of seven singers that included Anna Strada del Pò, a soprano who would be his leading lady through 1738, as well as the castrato Antonio Maria Bernacchi. With its revised financial schema, the Academy now had a far greater degree of dependence on the King. Handel's output for the 1729 season included *Lotario*, an opera about the death of Italy's Lothair II (the plot of which overlapped with *Ottone*); the satirical

Partenope, a delightful comedy about princes and princesses that manages to achieve some poignancy; and the pasticcio *Ormisda*, which drew on the arias of other composers with original recitative. In a cruel twist, only the latter proved popular during the season.

As a birthday present for Handel in 1732, Bernard Gates, Master of the Children of the Chapel Royal, presented three private performances of *Esther*, Handel's Cannons oratorio, which set in motion the composer's journey away from opera and toward unstaged musical drama.[4] These performances led to an unauthorized public performance of *Esther* in London, which in turn led Handel to produce an enlarged version of the work at the King's Theatre in 1732, sung in English with a largely Italian cast. While the private performances had been staged, the new (public) version was presented without action, given the prohibition of public staging of biblical drama in Britain—then by decree of the Bishop of London, Edmund Gibson, though the ban presaged Gibson by quite some time.

In May of 1732 another unauthorized performance of a Handel dramatic work, *Acis and Galatea*, was given at the Little Theatre in the Haymarket. Handel again wrote an expanded version in English and Italian and presented it as a serenata (a dramatic cantata normally composed for a particular celebration or person that took place outdoors at night) giving London two new musical forms in two months—oratorio and serenata—that could be used as an alternative to opera.

With the 1732–1733 season came new works and trouble. Handel's *Orlando* had its premiere in January, 1733, an opera

---

4 See Chapter 2, Handel's English Oratorios.

that masterfully depicted the madness of its hero by disregarding the expectations of Baroque operatic convention, notably through its use of irregular forms and limiting the *primo uomo*'s opportunities for improvisation. Handel's second English oratorio, *Deborah*, set to a biblical text from Judges, premiered in March of the same year. The same season saw the end of Handel's longstanding but turbulent collaboration with Senesino, who ultimately fractured the relationship in June (perhaps owing in the short term to the limited nature of the *Orlando* title role) by leaving Handel's company only to reengage with the Opera of the Nobility. In related news, Handel started to appear to others to be gaining too much power for a common musician, and a posse of nobility and gentry, led by Frederick, Prince of Wales, gathered to undermine Handel's monopoly of Italian opera in London. Handel's role as de facto controller of opera for the city with no aristocratic directors overseeing him was unacceptable to those who still saw musicians as servants.[5] Handel's position was also linked directly to the king, which made him a target for those who opposed the Whig government and sought to install Frederick as patriot king. Members of the opposition created the Opera of the Nobility, and picked up Senesino for the following season to boot, as well as many other leading opera singers. In keeping with the adage that all publicity is good publicity, the assault on Handel's hill was not entirely destructive, as it roused his supporters and gave him a tremendous boost in recognition as a musician.

---

5   Handel's life as a cosmopolitan celebrity and entrepreneur stands in stark contrast to the life of his contemporary J.S. Bach (1685–1750), provincial composer and servant to German aristocrats and the Lutheran church.

By the fall of that year, Handel had assembled a new opera company with a new castrato, Giovanni Carestini. After a slow start, Carestini gained admirers, and *Arianna in Creta*, which opened in January 1734, fared well against rival cross-town productions at Lincoln's Inn Fields. Handel produced *Parnasso in festa*, his only Italian serenata, for the wedding of the Princess of Wales and the Prince of Orange in March, 1734.

After Handel's five-year contract with Heidegger ended in 1734, the Nobility Opera took over the King's Theatre. Handel, however, had another venue available in John Rich's theatre at Covent Garden. Rich gave Handel two opera nights a week to balance out the plays that otherwise held the stage. The 1734–1735 season saw a revival of *Arianna in Creta* and *Oreste*, a pasticcio Handel created from previously written material with new recitatives and dances. He wrote two of his greatest operas in 1735—*Ariodante*, a romantic drama with technically difficult arias and modest scoring; and the emotionally rich allegory *Alcina*. In 1736, he again wrote music for a royal wedding—this time a light opera based on a Greek myth, *Atalanta*, and a wedding anthem, *Sing unto God*, for the Prince of Wales.

King Frederick and his wife attended the opening production of the 1736–1737 season, a revival of *Alcina*. Handel had three new operas for the season: *Arminio*, a return in style for Handel to a more heroic libretto; the entertaining *Giustino*, and the rather innocuous *Berenice*, as well as a refashioning of his first Italian oratorio, *Il trionfo del Tempo e della Verità*. A decline in quality and effort seen in these works pointed to Handel's then deteriorating health. In September 1737, he took a celebrated trip to the German spa city of Aachen

(Aix-la-Chapelle) for a successful cure in the vapor baths, an early account of which was relayed with fervor and arrives by way of Joseph Bennett's *Great Composers*:

> It was thought best for him to have recourse to the vapor baths at Aix-la-Chapelle, over which he sat three times as long as hath ever been the practice. Whoever knows anything of the nature of these baths, will, from this instance, form some idea of his surprising constitution. His sweats were profuse beyond what can well be imagined. His cure, from the manner as well as from the quickness with which it was wrought, passed with the nuns for a miracle. When, but a few hours from the time of his leaving the bath, they heard him at the organ in the principal church, as well as convent, playing in a manner so much beyond what they had ever heard or even imagined, it is not wonderful, that they should suppose the interposition of a higher power.

The demise of the Nobility Opera permitted Handel to return to the King's Theatre in the fall of 1737, where he wrote a virtuosic new opera spilling over with plot twists, *Faramondo*, for the upcoming season. This was followed by another pasticcio, *Alessandro Severo*, and then *Serse*, one of his best-regarded comic operas with short, bright arias and presciently modern situational scoring that finds the opera confidently holding the middle ground between farce and tragedy. A benefit concert that season featured *An Oratorio*, a pasticcio that blended church music and oratorio. Handel's reputation was on the rise again and he was put in good stead with the public, thanks in no small part to his financial help in the founding of the Fund for the Support of Decay'd Musicians (which exists today as the Royal Society of Musicians).

Financial difficulties with the King's Theatre during the following season (1738–1739) encouraged Handel to turn his attention to oratorio. The libretto for *Saul* was provided by Charles Jennens, a patron of the arts, a champion of Handel, editor of Shakespearean plays and a devout Christian. Jennens was Handel's greatest librettist and also furnished Handel with texts for the masque *L'Allegro, il Penseroso ed il moderato* (1740), and later, *Belshazzar* (1744). Of course, Jennens also designed the libretto for *Messiah* (1741). It is now considered likely that Jennens was also involved with Handel's other scriptural oratorio, *Israel in Egypt* (1738). For *Saul*, Jennens drew on the biblical account of King Saul (with Abraham Cowley's epic poem *Davideis* used as a secondary source). Saul's jealousy of the wartime success of David leads to his downfall and death in battle. *Saul* was the first oratorio that saw the effective coalescence of Handel's talent for writing estimable arias and choruses in combination with his sense of dramatic structure and gift for fashioning round characters. The oratorio includes the famous Dead March, a funeral anthem for Saul and his son, Jonathan, as well as some of Handel's best dramatic choral writing. The Dead March surprises by its use of a major key and achieves an uplifting sensibility without sacrificing gravitas.

The shift in entertainment at the King's Theatre from opera to oratorio and ode in 1739 was generally met with support, but the public missed the lighter feel of Italian opera. Covent Garden still provided opera while Handel moved to Lincoln's Inn Fields and presented a set of new Grand Concertos. The following season (1740–1741) saw the premiere of *Imeneo*, a modest but pristine drama taken from Greek mythology about Hymen's rise from Athenian to god of marriage, as well as *Deidamia*, Handel's last opera, a light treatment of Achilles' boyhood.

Handel's departure from Italian opera coincided with his departure from London for Dublin in 1741, where he put on two series of six concerts each of music from his English choral works, including *Saul* and *L'Allegro* at Dublin's newly opened Neale's new Musick-hall (only the door remains today) on Fishamble Street. *Messiah*, though it had been composed in London, concluded the Dublin season in 1742, with two performances benefiting three charities, which helped to allay any controversy over the oratorio's use of scriptural texts.

Success from the season spent in Dublin boosted Handel's confidence. He returned to London convinced of the merit of the oratorio form, which wedded operatic, choral, and orchestral elements, and was eager to test its mettle. Handel completed the oratorio *Samson* in London in 1742 with the help of librettist Newburgh Hamilton, who drew from Milton's *Samson Agonistes* as well as other, smaller Milton poems.

In 1743 Handel gave the first performance of *Samson* and the London premiere of *Messiah*, both at Covent Garden Theatre, establishing a springtime (Lenten) concert series that he would hold annually until the end of his life. *Samson* delighted audiences for its range of choral styles and arias and helped to position oratorio as opera's equal in the eyes of the public. *Messiah* did not fare as well, owing to outcry over the singing of Scripture in the theatre rather than the church; this panicked Handel to the extant that, without changing its title, he advertised *Messiah* in vague terms as "A New Sacred Oratorio."

Handel suffered a brief illness following the spring performances (owing largely to the *Messiah* controversy), but recovered mightily and penned *Semele*—a de facto opera performed as an oratorio for Theatre Royal's Lenten concert series—as well as a large-scale Te Deum and an anthem, "The King shall Rejoice," later in the year. These he followed with the oratorio *Joseph and his Brethren*, which was featured in the 1744 Lenten concerts along with *Semele* and the oratorios *Samson* and *Saul*. Next came *Hercules*, a "musical drama" written with librettist Rev. Thomas Broughton, who culled accounts of Hercules's death from Sophocles and Ovid. Handel then renewed his collaboration with Jennens for the oratorio *Belshazzar*. Jennens took for his subject the fall of the Babylonian king, and drew on the biblical account as well as writings by Herodotus and Xenophon's *Cyropaedia*.

Handel returned to the King's Theatre for the 1744–1745 season to present a series of oratorio concerts, which included performances of the opera *Hercules* as well as a revival of *Messiah*, the latter being received without incident, but not necessarily with success. A second Jacobite rebellion stymied the 1745–1746 oratorio season, though Handel did put together his *Occasional Oratorio*, which drew from *Israel in Egypt* and other previously composed works.

Handel's *Judas Maccabaeus*, a victory oratorio for William, Duke of Cumberland, premiered in April of 1747 at the Covent Garden Theatre. The oratorio relays the story of the revolt of the ancient Hebrews against Syrian occupiers and the Hebrews' eventual alliance with the Romans against them with help from their eponymous leader. The libretto is based on biblical episodes and Milton's version of the Psalms and was written by Rev. Thomas Morell, who would supply librettos for three additional Handel oratorios, including *Alexander Balus*, which Handel composed in the summer of the same year. The oratorios *Susanna* and *Solomon* were first performed in 1749 and mark a luxuriousness in Handel's music that would endure through the remainder of his oeuvre. *Solomon*, in particular, employs fuller orchestration than Handel's usual palette.

Messiah saw a revival in 1749 after a four-year hiatus—and has been performed every year since to present day. That same year in April Handel drew on *Messiah* for his anthem *How Beautiful are the Feet*, in celebration of the Peace of Aix-la-Chappelle, the treaty which ended the War of Austrian Succession. The celebration also saw the premiere of The Music for the Royal Fireworks, a large orchestral work which Handel wrote to accompany the celebration. In May, Handel began an important humanitarian relationship with London's Foundling Hospital—founded in 1739 as a children's home established for the "education and maintenance of exposed and deserted young children"—which would last to the end of his days and beyond. The charity benefit concert celebrating the newly constructed hospital chapel included the new Handel anthem, *Blessed are they That Considereth the Poor*, which became the Foundling Hospital Anthem. Handel was elected a governor of the hospital the next day, and would, upon his death ten years later, bequeath to the Hospital a copy of *Messiah*, which had been frequently performed there.

Handel's next oratorio, *Theodora*, was written in 1749, with Morell again serving as librettist. This work did not draw from biblical passages but rather from Robert Boyle's late seventeenth-century novel, *The Martrydom of Theodora and Didymus*, a tragic love story framed by the familiar struggle of Christians vs. Romans. *Theodora* was not well received, though it has made a return to form in recent years, and is now considered to be in the top tier of Handel's oratorios, which includes *Judas Maccabeus, Messiah, Saul,* and *Israel in Egypt.*

In 1750, at the age of 65, Handel wrote his will and went to Germany to see friends and relatives. He returned to London in 1751 and composed his last great orchestral work, the Organ Concerto in B-flat, and began work on the oratorio *Jephtha,* again with libretto by Morell. Handel had begun to lose his eyesight, however, and had to cease composing, returning to *Jephtha* at a slower pace later in the year. By 1753, Handel had become completely blind.

Despite his blindness, Handel continued to supervise oratorio seasons and perform organ concertos. His final oratorio season began in March of 1759 featuring a revised *Solomon.* Handel was unable to attend the performances due to poor health and following a final *Messiah* on April 6 was confined to bed. He dictated the last codicil to his will on April 11 and made several bequests, including £1,000 to the Fund for the Support of Decay'd Musicians. Handel died on April 14 and, per his request, was buried in Westminster Abbey. In a letter, Handel's friend James Smyth wrote: "He died as he lived—a good *Christian,*[6] with a true sense of his duty to God and man, and in perfect charity with all the world." A monument to Handel in the Abbey by the sculptor Roubiliac was completed in 1762. It depicts him with the open score of "I know that my Redeemer liveth" from *Messiah.*

---

6 The emphasis is Smyth's.

Chapter 2

*H*andel's English Oratorios

ORATORIO IS AN EXTENDED MUSICAL SETTING of a sacred, usually non-liturgical text. The term received its name from the Roman oratory, or prayer hall—in Latin, *oratio* means "prayer"—formed in the 1550s by St. Filippo Neri and used for informal spiritual gatherings. The roots of oratorio, however, stretch back to the settings of sacred texts in the Middle Ages as well as Medieval mystery plays, whose purpose was to provide education in key points of the Bible to a population that was largely illiterate or lacked access to the Good Book. Biblical texts were set to music and men were taught to sing them—chiefly to learn their verses. In the Renaissance and early Baroque period, dramatic and narrative text took the form of opera, and then, oratorio. Apart from a greater emphasis on the chorus, oratorio has, in form and style, historically reflected the opera of the time—with a notable lack of scenery, costume, and dramatic action. Oratorio is strictly a concert piece and deals solely with sacred subjects. Textually, sixteenth-century religious madrigals act as precursors to oratorio as well as settings of the Passion, *laude*, and motets. In Neri's oratory, *laude* (non-liturgical religious songs) were the spiritual exercises of choice, usually three- and four-part pieces, sometimes veering into more complex polyphony. Music historians see a direct evolution from the incorporation of narrative and dramatic texts within *laude* to the development of Italian oratorio. But it can also be argued that oratorio is a form that developed out of necessity, one which met the requirements of place (oratory) and taste (dramatic).

The early 1600s also saw the rise of Latin dialogues based on biblical stories in a monodic style (meaning music for a single voice or part). While these dialogues resembled future oratorios musically and textually, they were usually shorter and were included in larger books of motets, intended to be used alongside the motets in a church setting. Cavalieri's sacred opera, *Rappresentatione di Anima, et di Corpo*, premiered in 1600 at the Oratory of Chiesa Nuova in Rome and was notable for introducing the monodic style, while Anerio's sacred dialogue *Teatro armonico* (written in 1619) lay the real groundwork for oratory, which grew popular in Italy through a combination of the recent success of opera and the Church's prohibition of spectacles during Lent, making oratorio the only dramatic and musical option during this period. By the 1650s, two types of oratorio had developed: *oratorio volgare*, (i.e., vernacular), in Italian, usually in two musical sections, with examples including Carissimi's *Daniele* and Marazzoli's *S Tomaso*; and *oratorio latino*, in Latin, with Carissimi's *Jephte* (in one musical section) being the first masterpiece of that branch. The oratorio as we know it was established by 1660, and the form was popular in both oratories and secular surroundings through 1720. (Handel's *La resurrezione*, for instance, was performed at the Ruspoli residence in Rome.) Other oratorio composers of the period included Caldara, Gasparini, Alessandro Scarlatti (*Il regno di Maria Vergine assunta in cielo*), and Vivaldi (*Juditha triumphans*). Outside of Italy, the Italian oratorio was a Lenten substitute for opera at Roman Catholic courts in central Europe.

The 1700s saw the genre of "Oratorium," with German text, used in Lutheran services. Oratorium had its predecessors in composers from the mid-1600s who set nonbiblical text to music, resulting in the "oratorio Passion," most notably the Passions of Bach. The innovations of Oratorium included a more prominent use of the chorus by German composers—notably settings by Handel, Keiser, Mattheson, and Telemann of Brockes's famous poetic version of the Passion—than that of their Italian counterparts.

While he never referred to them as such, preferring terms such as "canticum," "historia," or "dialogue," Charpentier, a student of Carissimi, appears to have been the first French composer of oratorios. Few Frenchmen followed suit. In Italy and Vienna, *oratorio volgare*, which features solo singing, was heard through the late 1700s. In Dresden, the Lutheran oratorio functioned as a substitute for the cantata, and in concerts at Hamburg under the guidance of C. P. E. Bach and Telemann. Saying "God will not be angry with me for worshipping him in a cheerful manner," the late and joyful oratorios of Joseph Haydn (1732–1809), *The Creation* and *The Seasons*, show Handelian influence and reflect Haydn's experience with Handel's oratorios in London, when he attended the Handel Commemoration of 1791 at Westminster Abbey.

Composers who wrote from 1800 and beyond did not add much to the genre, but oratorio continued to hold a central place in the repertoire, particularly in music festivals in England and Germany that relied on large choral performances. Oratorios by Spohr (*Die letzten Dinge*) and Mendelssohn (*Elijah*) gained a place in the oratorio pantheon as well as the choral-society repertory, but beyond Mendelssohn the history of oratorio becomes a history of individual masterpieces rather than influential composers. Notable nineteenth- and twentieth-century oratorios include Berlioz's *L'enfance du Christ* (1854), Elgar's *The Dream of Gerontius* (1900), Schoenberg's *Die Jakobsleiter* (1922), Honegger's *Le roi David* (1923), and Walton's *Belshazzar's Feast* (1931).

While it had its predecessors, English oratorio was essentially Handel's creation. In fashioning the genre, Handel synthesized elements from Italian opera, the English masque and anthem, French classical drama, German Protestant oratorio, and Italian *opera seria* and *oratorio volgare*. Of course, even though Handel became a naturalized English citizen in 1726, his musical heritage draws on broader European traditions, which accounts not only for his broad taste, but also his broad appeal. For Handel, oratorio is a three-act dramatic work based on a biblical subject with a prominent use of the chorus performed in concert in a theatre rather than a church. Exceptions to Handel's usual structure of oratorio are *Israel in Egypt*, *Messiah*, and *Occasional Oratorio*, all of which employ nondramatic librettos. Freed from the staging restrictions of opera—usually considered a benefit to the concertgoer—oratorio permits a journey both more personal and cerebral. The librettos of Handel's oratorios, excepting

Messiah and *Theodora*, are based on the Old Testament, and even *Messiah* contains more text from the Old Testament than the New. The emphasis on the classical was reflected by Handel's choice of librettists, who did much to incorporate the technique and spirit of ancient Greek drama—further embraced by the dominant use of the chorus. It is notable that *Messiah* is not representative of Handel's English oratorios, in that the work itself has no action at all, no plot, no characters, and could be labeled reflective rather than dramatic. There were few Englishmen (Arne, Greene, Stanley) who attempted to follow in Handel's footsteps and master the oratorio form.

Esther (1732)[7]

Handel's form came about when his *Esther* (written in 1718) was prevented from being performed by Bishop of London Edmund Gibson's ban on staging biblical material. The libretto for the 1718 version of *Esther* is anonymous but draws heavily from Jean Racine's classical tragedy of the same name, importing aspects of Greek tragedy to the English oratorio, notably the importance—and central role—of the chorus. In the drama, the chorus is split into a group of Persian soldiers, led by Haman, the despotic Persian prince; and a group of Israelites, which supports Esther, queen of Persia, and Mordecai, a priest despised by Haman. Esther and her husband, Ahasuerus (king of the Persians), intervene on behalf of the Jews and Haman's plans of annihilation are

---

7 The year indicated for Handel's oratorios is the year of the premiere, not composition.

defeated, Haman is executed and Mordecai honored for saving the life of Ahasuerus. In addition to the prominence of the chorus, *Esther* establishes Handel's precedent for use of the Old Testament in English oratorio as well as taking tales of heroism for the work's subject.

Esther lay dormant for more than a decade following its composition until it was presented in a staged version in February 1732 in private performances at the Philharmonic Society and the Academy of Ancient Music. The title page of the printed libretto read: "Esther: an Oratorio; or Sacred Drama." The classification of oratorio was likely used here due to the work's religious nature. Following private performances, a public—and pirated—performance was announced in April of the same year. It is not known whether this production was staged or not. The announcement prompted Handel to declare on April 19 (a day before the pirated production was set to open) that his own presentation of the work would occur in May:

> By His MAJESTY's Command
> At the King's Theatre in the Hay-Market, on Tuesday the 2d Day of May, will be performed, the *Sacred Story of* ESTHER: an *Oratorio* in *English*. Formerly compos'd by Mr. *Handel*, and now revised by him, with several Additions, and to be performed by the best Voices and Instruments.
>
> N.B. There will be no Action on the Stage, but the House will be fitted up in a decent Manner, for the Audience. The Musick to be disposed after the Manner of the Coronation Service.[8]

---

8 *Daily Journal* (London) April 19, 1732, in Smither, A *History of the Oratorio Volume 2.*

With this announcement, Handel not only reclaimed *Esther* but also defined and cemented the form of English oratorio—and co-opted the Italian tradition of gussying up a concert hall for an oratorio performance (as had been the case with Handel's *La Resurrezione* in Rome in 1708). The restriction on staging for Handel's 1732 performance and use of continental traditions, however, were heavily influenced by Bishop Gibson, who considered the opera house an immoral venue and refused to permit a staged performance there of sacred subject matter that featured boy singers from the Chapel Royal (where Gibson was dean).

Handel's revised concert version included additions by librettist Samuel Humphreys, who would pen the librettos of Handel's next two oratorios. Humphreys added additional arias, recitatives, choruses and duets to the work. For the composer's part, the finale was shortened and the overture expanded. Many of the *da capo* arias (A–B–A form, that is, an aria where the first section is repeated following the second) lost their "B" and *da capo* sections, marking the beginning of Handel's journey away from use of the form for his oratorio arias. Handel also expanded *Esther's* orchestration to include percussion and additional brass and continuo. The revised *Esther* met with great success, was given six performances in May to full houses, and prompted Handel to compose two more oratorios the following year: *Deborah* and *Athalia*, the latter being Handel's first great oratorio.

Deborah (1733)

First, however, came *Deborah*. This oratorio, performed in the spring of 1733, was presented, like *Esther*, as a substitute for opera at the King's Theatre.

. . . on Saturday the 17th of March, will be performed,
DEBORAH: an *Oratorio*, or *Sacred Drama*, in *English*
Composed by Mr. Handel. And to be performed by a great
Number of the best Voices and Instruments. N.B. This is
the last Dramatick Performance that will be exhibited at
the King's Theatre till after Easter. The House to be fitted
up and illuminated in a new and particular Manner.[9]

As before, the announcement in London's *Daily Journal*
felt compelled to address audience expectations by giving
fair warning as to a lack of onstage scenery ("new and particular Manner"). In any case, *Deborah* failed at the box
office on opening night. Prices had been doubled and the
oratorio had been placed outside the subscription series,
making for a poor turnout and angering subscribers, some
of whom forced their way into the house notwithstanding.
Additional performances of *Deborah* at the King's Theatre
(at lower prices) received mixed reviews, with some finding
the hundred or so performers and singers magnificent and
others calling the spectacle excessive and noisy.

Humphrey's three-act libretto relates a conflict between
the Israelites and the Canaanites from the Book of Judges.
The chief Israelites are Deborah, Barak, Abinoam, and Jael,
led by three Israelite Women and the Chief Priest. As in
Esther, there are rival choruses—here, it's Israelite Priests
vs. Priests of Baal, with Sisara as the leading Canaanite.
Deborah, prophet and judge of Israel, compels Barak to
lead the Israelites against the Canaanites, prophesying
that the Israelites shall be the victors and that the leader
of the Canaanites, Sisara, shall die by a woman's hand.
Act II finds futile negotiation between the two peoples.

---

9 *Daily Journal* (London) March 12, 1733, in Smither, *A History of the Oratorio*
Volume 2.

In Act III, Deborah's prophesy comes to pass as the Canaanites are defeated and Jael kills Sisara as he sleeps in her tent. There is much rejoicing.

If the libretto is dramatically weak, the dramatic role of the opposing choruses is strong. There are as many choruses as arias in *Deborah*, and choruses frame all three acts. The chorus "All your boasts will end in woe" effectively joins an ensemble of leads (Deborah, Sisera, Barak and Baal's Priest) with the Israelite and Caananite choruses (a double chorus), the latter entering at the height of dramatic urgency. The music for *Deborah* is largely borrowed from Handel's previous works and as a result feels somewhat disjointed. Structurally, Handel here further limits use of the *da capo* form in his arias, an increasing trend in the oratorios that were to come.

Athalia *(1733)*

Handel's *Athalia*, labeled in its libretto as "An Oratorio: or Sacred Drama" was premiered in July of 1733 at a graduation ceremony ("Publick Act") at Oxford University and was well received. Like *Esther*, *Athalia*, too, was based on a tragedy by Racine (*Athalie*), which itself drew from a biblical story. Humphreys again served as librettist, here relating the story of Queen Athalia, whose hunger for power turns her away from Jehova and toward Baal, with disastrous consequences. In Act I of the oratorio, Athalia awakes from nightmares of being killed by a boy dressed as a priest of Judah. In visiting the temple to seek out the boy in her dreams (Act II), Athalia finds that the boy is real: he is Joas, king of the Israelites and is due shortly to be presented to his people by his parents,

Joad and Josabeth. Athalia hatches a plan to steal back to the temple within the hour and take Joas away. In Act III, Joas is presented as king of Judah and Athalia sees her plan thwarted when the commander of the army (Abner) refuses to do her bidding. Athalia realizes that Jehovah is victorious and prepares herself for impending death. The chorus offers celebrations of joy and thanks.

Most of the music for *Athalia* is new. An even more prudent use of the *da capo* aria (vis-à-vis *Deborah*) permits an easier buildup of dramatic tension, a trend that continues through *Saul* and *Samson*. This is all to say that the shortening of the aria from the *da capo* form allows the music to get out of the way of the action as it literally does not repeat itself. Another decision that improves Handel's burgeoning form here from a dramatic standpoint is the increased use of accompanied recitative rather than *secco* recitative ("dry," accompanied only by continuo), which accommodates a greater range of moods, emotional contextualizing and dramatic accent. With its increased flexibility in musical form and Handel's permissiveness to make use of his full arsenal of operatic and orchestral maneuvers, *Athalia* treads the widest emotional landscape yet within Handel's early ventures into English oratorio. An early aria praising Jehovah comes in a dance form and is followed by a chorus of praise in the form of a *passacaglia*. Later, mounting tension is depicted by the chorus in a Passion-like setting ("Tyrants would in impious throngs"). This is juxtaposed to a classic rage aria from the operatic tradition (Abner's "When storms the proud to terrors doom"). Following the storm, the tension subsides in a recitative by Joas, which is soothed by the accompaniment of strings.

Saul (1738)

After a five-year hiatus from oratorio, Handel was driven back to the form by economic forces when the King's Theatre could not draw in sufficient subscribers to hold a season (in 1738). It was during this period (1738–1745) that Handel would ultimately abandon opera for oratorio and create much of his best work for the form. Handel began work on *Saul* with librettist Charles Jennens only days prior to the cancellation of the season. Like *Athalia*, the oratorio tells the story of an Israelite leader alienated from his people by a tragic flaw. Here, King Saul's pride and envy lead him to ruin. Running parallel to Saul's struggle with his shortcomings (and with those around him) is the struggle of the Israelites against their enemies. *Saul* opens with a triumphant chorus—The People of Israel, whose voices have a central role throughout—singing in celebration of David vanquishing Goliath. Saul, too, praises David and offers him his younger daughter, Merab, in marriage. David and Saul's son Jonathan form a close friendship. Time passes (marked by a sinfonia) and then a chorus of Israelite women welcome Saul and David home from war, singing praises to both, but praising David above the king. Thus it is the chorus who innocuously sets in motion Saul's tragic downfall. The king fixates upon the geometric discrepancy between the chorus's praises: "Saul, who has thy thousands slain, / Welcome . . ." and "David his ten thousands slew / Ten thousand praises are his due." Merab urges David to soothe Saul's temper, but David's efforts are in vain and Saul flies into a rage, launching his javelin at him before David makes his escape. Saul orders Jonathan to kill David, but, in Act II, Jonathan instead warns David of the plot against him and informs him that Merab has now been promised to another. Jonathan pleads with Saul to spare David, and Saul pretends to reconcile, offering David his older daughter, Michal, in marriage. But once they are married, Saul secretly hopes that David will be killed in war with the Philistines. When David returns unscathed, Saul, enraged again, makes two more attempts on his life, and, when questioned by his son, attempts to kill him, too. In Act III, Saul seeks out the Witch of Endor and begs the Witch to call Samuel back from the dead in order to benefit from his counsel. The Witch grants his request and the ghost of Samuel tells Saul that (1) the kingdom will be given to David, (2) Saul and his sons will perish, and (3) Israel will fall to the Philistines. The prophecy is fulfilled. Saul attempts suicide and then convinces an Amalekite to finish the job. David, on learning the Amalekite's nationality, has him killed. Handel's celebrated "Dead March" and elegy follow for Saul and the chorus concludes the oratorio, encouraging David to pursue his destiny.

Following in the footsteps of *Athalia* from a dramatic standpoint, *Saul* victoriously weds musical and dramatic elements (only four of the oratorio's thirty arias are in *da capo* form) and further liberates itself from much of the convention of *opera seria*. As a tragic figure, Saul is vividly sketched—largely through others or by means of recitative. Saul himself has only three arias, fewer than David and Jonathan, atypical for a title role in the *opera seria* or *oratorio volgare* tradition. This oratorio is framed by the chorus, who opens *Saul* with "Epinicion, or Song of Triumph" and closes the work with "Elegy on the Death of Saul and Jonathan." Both choruses come in the wake of battle, the first expressing victory, the latter expressing grief that is somewhat blunted with hope for the future.

The orchestration for *Saul* is quite large, and includes flute, oboe, bassoon, trumpet, trombone, timpani, harp, theorbo, strings, two organs, harpsichord, and an inventive use of carillon (a keyboard that sounds bells with hammers), an instrument featured in the choruses that provoke Saul's jealousy and rage. A letter from Jennens in September 1738 reveals that Handel had come into possession of the carillon while composing *Saul*:

> Mr. Handel's head is more full of maggots than ever. I found yesterday in his room a very queer instrument which he calls carillon (Anglice, a bell) and says some call it a Tubalcain, I suppose because it is both in the make and tone like a set of Hammers striking upon anvils. 'Tis played upon with keys like a Harpsichord and with this Cyclopean instrument he designs to make poor Saul stark mad.[10]

Israel in Egypt (1739)

This work, first performed in the spring of 1739, likely grew from an anthem to a three-act oratorio and was later published as a two-act oratorio, its most common arrangement when performed today. The work initially did not fare well, owing to a prominence of the chorus beyond audience expectations and, of greater impact, an offending of religious sensitivities due to Handel's use of a libretto that was taken nearly verbatim from Scripture. The oratorio was performed at the

---

10 Jennens to Lord Guernsey, September 19, 1738, in Smither, *A History of the Oratorio Volume 2.*

King's Theatre, and many Londoners questioned whether the venue was appropriate for Scripture. A letter that defended Handel's use of the venue for such a purpose appeared in the *London Daily Post* following the final performance of *Israel in Egypt*, and asserted that the "Entertainment" was the "noblest Adoration and Homage paid to the Deity that ever was in one . . ."[11] This letter marked the beginning of a movement of defending the Handelian oratorio on spiritual grounds while downplaying the genre as theatre or entertainment. Such a defense greatly contributed to Handel's image as a sacred composer and moralist rather than musical dramatist. *Israel in Egypt* and *Messiah* are the only two of Handel's oratorios based on nondramatic biblical texts, an abnormality for Handel's oratorio output and a significant departure from the European musical traditions of the time.

Israel in Egypt culls from Exodus and Psalms. Part I relates the oppression of the Israelites in Egypt, the plagues that visited the Egyptians, and the Israelites' crossing of the Red Sea. Part II features songs of praise sung by Moses and the Israelites following their escape from Egypt. There are no individual roles for Moses or others. The librettist for *Israel* is unknown, and may have been Handel himself. The music is nearly entirely choruses and could easily be labeled an anthem, or group of anthems. The choruses (with large orchestra) are widely varied in their texture and text painting—chordal, fugal, pastoral and dance—accounting for the work's present-day popularity despite its problematic and unbalanced nature. The *da capo* form, it should be noted, is completely absent from *Israel's* arias.

---

11 *London Daily Post*, April 18, 1739

Messiah (1742)

Messiah was a success in its 1742 Dublin premiere, where a review described it as "the most finished piece of music." But the oratorio did not fare as well in London, where it caused outcry for its use of Scripture in the theatre. *Messiah* went underground briefly, and was performed without its proper title until 1750, when it was performed in the chapel of Foundling Hospital. The annual series there helped cement the popular conception that *Messiah*—and Handel's other oratorios—could be considered sacred music appropriate for church performance. Though *Messiah* and *Israel* are both non-dramatic, *Messiah* is closer to Handel's accustomed oratorio balance between solos and choruses; ultimately, the chorus remains even more prominent than in his dramatic oratorios. *Messiah's* choruses are more wide-ranging than those in *Israel*, with a creative mix of fugal, chordal, and contrapuntal styles. Only two of *Messiah's* arias ultimately retain their *da capo* status following Handel's revisions, while the arias and duets reflect the style of Handel's other dramatic oratorios and operas, with a third of them in dance form. The orchestral means for *Messiah* are modest: continuo and strings, with occasional trumpet, oboe, and timpani. *Messiah's* history, libretto and music are discussed in Chapters 3, 4 and 5 of this book, respectively.

From the perspective of oratorio, it is essential again to note that *Messiah*, though it is Handel's most popular oratorio, is by no means representative of the composer's work in that form. In all of his other oratorios, save *Israel* and *Messiah*, the chorus's role is second to that of the soloists. Handel's only further deviation from dramatic oratorio would come when he penned *Occasional Oratorio*.

Samson (1743)

Samson enjoyed the best first run yet of any of Handel's oratorios, with eight performances at the Theatre Royal in Covent Garden in February 1743. The libretto of Samson was written by Newburgh Hamilton, who, a fan of Milton, had seen Handel's setting of that author's L'Allegro and Il Penseroso and decided Handel might be just the man for an oratorio of Milton's Samson Agonistes. Notes Hamilton in the introduction to his libretto:

> . . . But as Mr. Handel had so happily inroduc'd here Oratorios, a musical Drama, whose Subject must be Scriptural, and in which the Solemnity of Church-Musick is agreeably united with the most pleasing Airs of the Stage: It would have been an irretrievable Loss to have neglected the Opportunity of that great Master's doing Justice to this Work . . .[12]

In terms of its text, Hamilton's libretto is far more Milton than Bible. In addition to Samson Agonistes, Hamilton paraphrased from 14 other poems by Milton. He also added a chorus of Philistines to oppose Milton's chorus of Israelites. By no means reflective to the degree of Messiah, Samson remains a far less dramatic oratorio than the likes of Saul or Athalia. The libretto's theme is Samson's spiritual development, from remorse for past sins and resentment at mistreatment to the tragic fulfillment of his divine destiny, all symbolized in the libretto by a journey from darkness into light—from an eclipsed sun (Samson's aria "Total eclipse") to a rising one (Samson's "Thus when the sun").

---

12 Burrows, Donald. Master Musicians: Handel.

The dramatic development of Samson's spiritual condition is revealed in dialogues that Samson, blind and bound, has with those who visit him. A festival opening the oratorio features the Philistines (reminiscent of the opening of *Saul*), with Samson lamenting his present torment. He is visited by his friend, Micah, a chorus of Israelites, and his father, Manoah, who is negotiating his ransom and release. Samson holds out hope that Jehovah might use him to take revenge on the Philistines. Samson is next visited by his wife, Dalila, and a chorus of Virgins. She attempts to make peace with him, without success. Harapha, the Philistine champion, visits next, reveling in Samson's misfortune, and eventually persuading him to attend the feast of Dagon. Samson accepts with the hope of destroying his tormentors and their temple. He does, and Samson dies in triumph. A lament and Dead March follow, and the end of the oratorio, like the beginning, is reminiscent of *Saul*. Lamentation from the chorus is soon overtaken by praise to Jehovah: "Samson like Samson fell—ruin is left: to him eternal fame."

Samson stands out for its keen match of music with emotion. "Torments, alas" finds Samson entering slowly in a minor key, unaccompanied after an orchestral introduction, emphasizing his loneliness. The manipulative Dalila is infused with transparent charm in her aria "With plaintive notes and am'rous moan," her motives mocked in imitation by the orchestra. Samson is all wrath in the duet with Harapha, "Go baffled coward," but when he makes the decision to attend the festival, his aria "Thus when the sun from's wat'ry bed" reveals a calm spiritual side, at odds with the raging and bitter captive that began the oratorio. The two choruses (Israelites and Philistines) tend to be given brief and plain settings, but they are prominent throughout with numerous appearances, and their narration proves essential to the unfolding of the drama. A fairly large orchestra—with woodwinds, brass, timpani, harpsichord and organ—is belied by remarkably light orchestration, a Handelian trademark.

Joseph and His Brethren (1744)

This oratorio was composed in 1743 and premiered in Covent Garden in the spring of 1744. It had a decent debut, was revived in four subsequent seasons, but has been largely forgotten over the centuries. The libretto was written by Rev. James Miller, who then had some comedies, satires and ballad operas under his belt, but no oratorio. *Joseph*, based on a biblical story from the Book of Genesis, would be Miller's first and last attempt at an oratorio libretto. In Act I, Joseph find himself in prison. He is summoned from his cell to interpret Pharaoh's dreams. Joseph's success in dream analysis lands him a plum position in Pharaoh's administration. Asenath, daughter of Potiphera the High Priest, falls in love with Joseph and they are married. In Act II, it is now seven years later and Joseph's brother, Simeon, has been in prison for a year and is being held there until his brothers return to Egypt. Joseph questions Simeon about his father and his brothers, particularly his youngest brother, Benjamin. The brothers then arrive: Benjamin, Reuben, and Judah. Joseph questions them, too, again with special attention to Benjamin. In Act III, the brothers are arrested on suspicion of stealing a silver cup, which to Benjamin's surprise is found in his bag. Joseph orders Benjamin sent to prison, but Simeon intervenes, offering to take his place, pleading that

Benjamin is the only remaining son of Jacob and Rachel—and his father's dearest son. Joseph is touched, and reveals his identity, asking his brothers to forgive his ruse, which he describes as a test of loyalty to Benjamin. They do and the oratorio closes with a rejoicing anthem.

Miller's libretto is weak due to its lack of drama, motivation, inspired language, and imagery. The oratorio is musically weak, too, perhaps because of what Handel was given to work with. Highlights include a stark aria from Joseph within his prison cell ("Be firm my soul") and Simeon's moving recitative from his own prison cell in Act II ("Where are these Brethren"). The chorus alternates in representation of the Egyptians and Joseph's brothers—and is used judiciously. One interesting note: Handel manages to transform the Dead March from *Samson* into a grand march during the procession in the wedding scene.

Belshazzar (1745)

Handel experienced a rough season in 1745 and had to cut his losses at the expense of *Belshazzar*, which saw only three performances in the spring of that year. The reasons for a shortened season stem either from the poor quality of the singers, the then poor quality of Handel's health, or some balance of the two. *Belshazzar* never really attained popularity and perhaps merits more attention. Charles Jennens' libretto, based on the Book of Daniel and supplemented with the writings of Herodotus and Xenophon, takes as its theme a kingdom in decline. The oratorio is set during the final day of Babylon. Nitocris, mother of Belshazzar, the tyrant king of Babylon, opens the oratorio with a reflection on the contrasting nature of the vanity of man and the unchanging nature of God. Cyrus, prince of Persia and instrument of God, is laying siege to Babylon, and plans to divert the Euphrates and take Babylon through the dry riverbed when the Babylonians are drunk at the feast of Sesach, the god of wine. In captivity, the prophet Daniel predicts the freeing of the Israelites. Belshazzar proclaims the feast and orders the sacred vessels from the Jerusalem temple be used to honor Sesach. This will prove to be a poor decision. At the end of Act I, a chorus of Israelites predicts the wrath of God. In Act II, Cyrus and his army prepare to take the city. When Belshazzar and his men drink from the sacred vessels, a disembodied hand appears and makes supernatural writing on the wall.[13] None of the Wise Men called to decipher it can read the writing. Nitocris urges Belshazzar to call for Daniel, who interprets the writing as foretelling the end of Belshazzar's reign. Cyrus enters the city at the close of Act II. In Act III Cyrus is victorious, freeing the Israelites. The Israelites sing a closing anthem praising God.

Jennens' dramatic libretto is quite strong and he builds on the immediacy of the oratorio by providing copious stage descriptions in lieu of narration. Indeed, the banquet scene is completely operatic in that Belshazzar and the chorus cry out as the hand writes on the wall, symbolized by staccato strings. Only the stage descriptions reveal what is taking place. The music is thus reactive rather than suggestive, pushing at the boundaries of the oratorio form. Given that the stage directions are essential for comprehension, here the case could

---

13 Both the expression "the writing on the wall" as a portent of doom and the attribution of the ability to "read the writing on the wall" to someone who can foresee an inevitable decline originated in the Book of Daniel.

even be made that *Belshazzar* is more opera performed in the manner of an oratorio than operatic oratorio.

Belshazzar shows Handel as master of characterization. The tyrant king is portrayed as boasting and vain through arias that are crafted as drinking songs ("Let festal joy triumphant reign," "Let the deep bowl thy praise confess," and "I thank thee, Sesach"). His character stands in contrast to Cyrus, who sings with humility and pious righteousness. The arias of Gobrias, a general to Cyrus who seeks vengeance for his son's murder at the hand of Belshazzar, express his seemingly disparate emotions of joy and sadness at the capture of Babylon, a city Gobrias deserted to escape tyranny. Daniel's character is static, but displays a calmness and a stalwart faith throughout. Belshazzar's mother, Nitocris, is painted as a loving and saddened voice of reason, pleading with her son in vain to consider his actions. Her opening recitative ("Vain, fluctuating state of the human empire") and following aria ("Thou, God most high") make for an elegant and philosophical reflection on the state of the universe. In Act III, her opening aria ("Alternate hopes and fears") beautifully captures her conflicted state toward her son's misdeeds. The arias of *Belshazzar* come in a variety of forms—*da capo*, non-*da capo*, strophic, binary and through-composed. The chorus is large and widely used, adopting different modes (not entirely consistent or convincing) to represent the Babylonians, Jews, and Persians.

Occasional Oratorio (1746)

Following the victory of the Duke of Cumberland over Prince Charles, Handel wrote and performed *Occasional Oratorio* in support of the Hanoverian monarchy. His three other war-themed oratorios that followed (*Judas Maccabeus, Alexander Balus,* and *Joshua*) could also be considered "occasional," since they, too, were written in the wake of and in celebration of military victories.

The oratorio was first performed in Covent Garden in 1746. The identity of the librettist is uncertain, but is likely Rev. Thomas Morrell. The libretto itself is pulled largely from Scripture, and, like *Israel in Egypt* and *Messiah,* is nondramatic. Parts I and II are mostly from Milton's translations of Psalms, while Part III includes text (and music) from *Esther, Israel,* and the anthem *Zadok the Priest,* in addition to new material. Distinct from Handel's other two nondramatic oratorios, there is no story here, and *Occasional Oratorio* can be reasonably labeled an anthem. Part I deals with war and God's vengeance, Part II with forthcoming peace, and Part III with praise of God for victory. The orchestra helps establish a martial theme with a heavy brass section and timpani—in addition to oboes, strings, continuo, harpsichord, and organ. There are fourteen choruses, with seven newly composed for the oratorio. Of these, the heavily contrapuntal "Hallelujah" is a standout. Within the arias, emphasis is placed on expression of heroism, patriotism, and vengeance. This is heard in the bass recitative "Why do the gentiles tumult and the nations muse a vain thing," the text of which is Milton's translation of the same psalm set in the *Messiah* aria "Why do the nations so furiously rage." Peace also makes an appearance with the pastoral tenor aria "Jehovah is my shield."

Judas Maccabaeus (1747)

Judas was ultimately given six performances in the 1747 season and remained popular both during Handel's lifetime and after his death. The libretto was written by Rev. Thomas Morell for the occasion of the Duke of Cumberland's victory in Scotland and draws primarily from the Book of Maccabees as well as from Flavius Josephus's *Antiquities of the Jews*. This oratorio is dramatic, though the only named personages are the titular hero and Judas's brother, Simon. In Act I, Judas laments the death of his father, Mattathias. Simon, feeling the spirit of the Lord, declares it God's will that Judas lead Israel. The people rally to Judas, who will lead them in their war for freedom. Act II finds the Israelites celebrating victory over the Syrians when The Messenger then warns of fresh attacks from Syria. The Israelites' morale is low, but Judas rallies them for another battle, while Simon remains to purify the temple of enemy sacrifices to heathen gods. Act III opens with the Feast of Lights. The Messenger returns with news of Judas's victories. Judas enters and orders the Israelites to prepare burial rites for fallen soldiers. Eupolemus arrives from Rome with an agreement assuring Judea's independence. There is much rejoicing.

While the libretto is a clear vehicle for Handel to compose victory music, some of the best music comes from the opening scene of lamentation, notably the chorus "Mourn, ye afflicted children," which is a funeral march, and the chorus "For Sion lamentation make," which employs a gentle lulling rhythm and effective rhetorical repetition. But most of the music is martial in its tone. Here, unlike *Occasional Oratorio*, Handel saves his trumpets and timpani for climactic use: Judas's aria "Sound the alarm." Other contrasts to bellicose chutzpah include arias of liberty and a fine duet, "Come ever smiling liberty." A further break from patriotism comes with "Father of Heav'n," a gentle and elegant hymn.

Alexander Balus (1748)

Handel hoped to match the popularity of *Judas* with this sequel but fell short. It saw three revivals in 1748, two in 1754 and very few since. The story of Alexander Balus falls directly after that of Judas Maccabaeus in the Book of Maccabees, upon which Morell based his libretto, along with verse from Milton and Shakespeare and Handel's earlier oratorios. Act I opens on the Asiates celebrating a victory that has installed Alexander as king of Syria. He makes a treaty with Jonathan, chief of the Jews, between their two peoples. Ptolomee, king of Egypt, and Cleopatra, Ptolomee's daughter, congratulate Alexander. Cleopatra and Alexander fall in love. The act closes with the Israelites singing praise to God. Alexander and Cleopatra are about to be married at the beginning of Act II, when an informer (falsely) claims that Jonathan plots against the throne. Alexander rejects the notion. Ptolomee then reveals in an aside that he plans to dethrone Alexander. In Act III, Ptolomee has his mercenaries kidnap Cleopatra as part of a harebrained plan to install the young Demetrius on the Persian throne. Alexander calls in Jonathan to join him in war against Ptolomee, who in turn tries to coerce his daughter to take his side against Alexander. During the war, a messenger informs Cleopatra that Jewish forces are victorious but that Alexander and Ptolomee have been killed. Cleopatra prays to Isis for *deus ex machina*, Jonathan meditates on the mysterious ways of God, and the Israelites sing praise to the eternal King.

This libretto vies for weakest among Handel's oratorios. There is little drama, no symbolic overlap in the love story and the Israelites' devotion to the true God, and Alexander is not a well fleshed out character, much less a tragic hero. Cleopatra is a bright spot and a fascinating character within the drama's final act. She is given a lush, pastoral Act-III aria in the garden ("Here amid the shady woods"), which is interrupted by her kidnappers, leading to a theatrical and musically compelling struggle. Cleopatra's scene with Ptolomee reveals a complex father-daughter relationship, which leads to a beautiful recitative mourning her father's coercion ("Shall Cleopatra ever smile again") and later, her death wish upon learning that her husband has been killed ("O take me from this hateful light"). When she learns of her father's death, Cleopatra's progression from despondency to withdrawal is given a simple and understated musical setting. The shift to Cleopatra as the oratorio's focus earns the chorus's finale its minor key. *Alexander* is ultimately closer in style to Handel's operas, with ten *da capo* arias and a minimal role for the chorus.

Joshua (1748)

First performed in Covent Garden in March of 1748, *Joshua* was given four more performances that month and an additional fourteen during the remainder of Handel's life. It continues to receive occasional performances. This despite another woeful libretto from Rev. Morell, based on the Book of Joshua, which would appear to be another attempt to tap into the magic jingoistic formula of *Judas*. Act I begins with the Israelites thanking God and praising Joshua for their safe passage through the Jordan river. An angel then appears to Othniel, a warrior, and Joshua, saying that Jericho will fall by Joshua's hand. Joshua calls the Israelites to arms. The act closes with a love scene between Othniel and Achsah, daughter of Joshua's military commander, Caleb. Othniel then goes off to war with the intention of returning and asking Caleb for his daughter's hand in marriage. The chorus wishes him Godspeed. In Act II, Joshua, now at the walls of Jericho with his army, issues the order to "Sound the shrill trumpets, shout, and blow the horns." The Israelites do so, and the walls tumble. The Israelites celebrate Passover, lament a defeat at the city of Ai, and are victorious over the Canaanites. A major part of Act III is made up of thanksgiving for victories. With only the city of Debir remaining to be conquered, Caleb promises his daughter to he who leads the final battle. Othniel volunteers, returns victorious (accompanied by the famous strains of "See the conqu'ring hero comes") and wins Achsah. The final hallelujah chorus reminds the audience: "The great Jehovah is our awful theme."

Act II features a compelling chorus, "Glory to God," that juxtaposes solo passages from Joshua interspersed with chordal "shouts" from the chorus describing the falling walls of Jericho.[14] More text painting follows, with strings and continuo agitatedly evoking "nations tremble at the sound" and "tempests roar," with timpani and trumpets rumbling over "Heav'n thunders." Handel wrote fourteen choruses for *Joshua*, closer to his usual number than written in the previous "occasional" oratorios (*Alexander, Judas* and *Occasional Oratorio*). The orchestration for *Joshua* is varied, astute, and compelling throughout.

---

14 Haydn was impressed with this chorus when he heard a performance of *Joshua* in 1791.

Solomon (1749)

Handel would leave his martial "occasional" oratorios for his final four works in the genre. These late-period works differed from the previous oratorios and also from one another. *Solomon* displays some lingering patriotism. This oratorio was composed in May of 1748 and saw its premiere in Covent Garden in March of 1749.

The anonymous libretto pulls from the Books of Kings and Book of Chronicles, as well as Josephus's *Antiquities of the Jews*. In Act I, a chorus of Priests, a Levite, Solomon, the high priest Zadok and a chorus of Israelites participate in a ceremony dedicating the temple. In a scene that recalls the Italian genre of *oratorio erotico*, Solomon and his Queen extol the sexual pleasures of marriage. A love duet follows, and then an aria from Zadok urging the King to "indulge thy faith" [wink, wink]. The final number of Act I is the chorus's "May no rash intruder disturb their soft hours," dubbed the Nightingale Chorus for the imitative nature of the final line in which nightingales lull the couple to sleep. Act II features Solomon's judgments, as two Harlots lay claim to the same baby and ask Solomon to rule. Solomon orders the child to be divided in half. The Second Harlot praises the decision, while the First Harlot would rather give the child up than see it killed. Solomon explains that he wished only "to trace with art / The secret dictates of the human heart" and awards the child to the First Harlot, who must be the true mother. The chorus praises Solomon's wisdom. In Act III Solomon displays the wealth of his kingdom to the visiting Queen of Sheba. He orders music that rouses each passion in a separate air: sweet music, martial, a lament, and then a calm after a storm. The Queen pays tribute to Solomon's aesthetic and to Solomon in the form of gold, gems, and balsam. The chorus and others praise them both. The Queen bids farewell, and she and Solomon sing a duet of mutual respect.

We can view this oratorio as a continuation of the "occasional" series for its function as a thinly veiled glorification of King George II. But this is no martial work, and the words and music are at a higher artistic level than the "occasionals." *Solomon's* characters are on the one hand symbolic: Solomon as ideal monarch; his Queen, conjugal love; Zadok, orthodox religion; Queen of Sheba, the respect of foreign power. Yet a humanist side, too, is found in the love scene between Solomon and his queen and the scene of the two harlots. The chorus is a major force in *Solomon*, large in number (a double chorus) and essential to the story. The four choruses that make up the Act-III masque are delightful in their contrivances to shift musical gears at Solomon's whim in order to impress the Queen of Sheba. Employing flute, oboe, bassoon, horn, and trumpet plus timpani, strings, harpsichord, and organ, *Solomon* is one of Handel's most elaborately and meticulously orchestrated oratorios.

Susanna (1749)

Premiered in Covent Garden in February of 1749, *Susanna* was performed four times in its first season, revived once by the composer in 1759, and has been largely neglected since Handel's death. The libretto is again anonymous—given the parallels between *Susanna* and *Solomon*, it is likely that the same author wrote both—and draws from the Book of Daniel. Susanna is married to Joacim, and the oratorio opens with the couple reflecting on the joys of married love.[15] Susanna's husband must leave the city for a week, giving the opportunity for The First and Second Elder to reveal their lust for Susanna. The two geezers hatch a plan to sexually assault her. The final chorus of Act I warns the two elders that they are observed by Heaven and shall be punished. In Act II, Joacim is homesick and misses his wife. Susanna, meanwhile, is in the garden with her Attendant, who leaves to procure ointments while Susanna bathes in a pool. The elders approach and make aggressive advances, which she rejects. As revenge, the elders call a chorus of Jews and claim they have seen Susanna in an act of adultery with a youth who has (conveniently) escaped. Joacim learns of the accusation and returns home. Act III opens with the decree by the chorus of Jews that Susanna has been found guilty and is to be put to death. However, a young man in the crowd, Daniel, proclaims that Susanna is innocent and demands the verdict be reversed. A Judge permits a new trial with Daniel as Susanna's defender. Daniel questions the elders separately, asking under which tree the crime was committed. Their stories don't line up and Susanna is declared innocent; the elders, guilty. Joacim and Susanna's father, Chelsias, enter and praise her fidelity. The chorus sings praises to the value of a virtuous wife.

Handel finds further kinship here with Italy's *oratorio erotico*, more so than *Solomon*, where sexuality was confined to a single episode. Yet the passion of the old men for the young vixen was a source of humor in the comic opera of Handel's day, and Handel's musical settings here bend more to comedy than they do to passion. As a result, the moralizing of the

---

15 Cf. *Solomon*.

chorus seems out of place. The light operatic quality of the work otherwise reigns, with a large number of *da capo* arias (a scheme more operatic than oratorio-like), a scant use of the chorus, and orchestrations that drift to dance forms and pastoral settings. The two elders are painted broadly, with a mock-heroic fanfare aria wherein the First Elder tries to rally himself to action. The Second Elder is given two mock-serious arias ("The oak that for a thousand years" and "The torrent that sweeps in its course") with obvious innuendo.

Theodora (1750)

Though its nonbiblical subject matter and musical subtlety made it box-office poison, *Theodora* was Handel's favorite of his own oratorios. Regardless, it was and remains seldom performed. Rev. Thomas Morell crafted the libretto from a historical novel, Robert Boyle's *The Martyrdom of Theodora and of Didymus*, and from Corneille's drama *Théodore Vierge et Martyre*. The oratorio pits Christians against heathens and opens with Valens, tyrant prefect of Antioch, proclaiming a celebration of Diocletian, which calls for all residents of Antioch to make a sacrifice to Jove. Didymus, a Roman officer and Christian sympathizer, pleads with Valens to permit conscientious objection to Romans who, though loyal, do not acknowledge Roman Gods. Didymus also appeals to his superior officer, Septimius, who ultimately refuses to disobey a direct order from Valens. Theodora, a Christian of noble birth, rejects the proclamation despite the risk of mortal peril. Septimius warns her that punishment will entail serving as a prostitute in the temple of Venus. Didymus promises to rescue her. Act II finds Valens and a chorus of

Heathens sacrificing to Jove and other gods in anticipation of the pleasures of Venus. Valens warns Septimius that Theodora has one final opportunity to sacrifice to Jove or be raped by the guards. Alone in prison, Theodora comforts herself in heavenly thoughts. Didymus confesses to Septimius that he is a Christian and is in love with Theodora, and convinces Septimius not to block his attempt at rescue. He enters the prison and initially startles Theodora in his helmeted guise. Didymus then reveals his identity, convinces Theodora to exchange clothes, and the two make their escape. In Act III, the Christian chorus rejoices at Theodora's escape. When a Messenger informs Theodora that Didymus has been captured and is facing the death penalty, Theodora goes to the court and offers her life in exchange. After Didymus and Theodora compete for the death sentence, Valens, in a perversion of Solomon-like justice, awards a death penalty to each. They are led away to execution and Irene, Theodora's Christian friend, along with the chorus of Christians, sings praise of divine love and prays for Didymus' and Theodora's martyrdom.

For *Theodora*, Handel made his only venture into Hagiography, the biography of saints or venerated persons. Hagiography was a common starting point for much of the late Baroque *oratorio volgare*, and Theodora had been taken as the subject of previous oratorios in Italy. *Theodora* is also Handel's sole dramatic English oratorio based on a Christian subject, with *Messiah*, his other Christian English oratorio, employing a nondramatic libretto. Musically, *Theodora* finds kinship with *Messiah* and with Handel's final oratorio, *Jephtha*, for its reflective nature. In keeping with that spirit of reflection, the oratorio contains a great number of *da capo* arias (13 out of 25).

An examination of Act II reveals an effective juxtaposition of contrasts and dramatic build. Two dancelike opening choruses frame an aria from Valens ("Wide spread his name"), a praise of the Roman emperor filled with fanfare. The second scene, Theodora's prison scene, blots out the light of the previous, with two arias and two recitatives, all presented with increasing levels of despair until Theodora's final aria, "Oh that on wings I could rise," wherein her despair is conquered. The next scene features subtly aligned arias from Didymus and Septimius that convey their distinctive stances. Scene four shifts to Irene, whose recitative and aria express her concern for Theodora's well being. The act's dramatic climax occurs in scene five, Theodora and Didymus's prison-break scene. Didymus's aria ("Sweet rose and lily, flow'ry form") is given a striking change in tenor with Theodora's plea for death ("The pilgrim's home"). This request is unquestionably rejected by Didymus ("Forbid it, Heaven!"). A plaintive parting duet closes the scene ("To thee, thou glorious son of worth"), given a rich orchestral accompaniment. Handel is said to have preferred the mighty scene-six chorus that closes the act—depicting Jesus's restoration of life to a widow's son—even to *Messiah*'s "Hallelujah" chorus.

Jephtha *(1752)*

Handel's final English oratorio[16] *Jephtha* was first performed at Covent Garden in February 1752. It saw a total of seven performances during the remainder of Handel's life and has

---

16 *The Triumph of Time and Truth*, performed in 1757, is sometimes credited with this distinction, but the work contains very little—if any—new music.

been performed frequently since his death. Rev. Thomas Morell's libretto is based on a story from the Book of Judges, and was the librettist's favorite oratorio of those he penned. Morell introduced changes and additional characters to the story, and much like his work with *Alexander Balus*, infused the libretto with text from other authors, including Milton. The oratorio opens with Zebul and his brothers recalling their half-brother Jephtha from exile—originally imposed because he was the bastard son of a whore—and calling on him to lead the Israelites against the oppressor Ammonites. Jephtha agrees provided that he retains his leadership role after the war. Jephtha's wife, Storgè, reflects on her husband's departure; Iphis, daughter of Jephtha, and the soldier Hamor declare their love for each other before the latter departs for war. Jephtha then vows that, if victorious, he will sacrifice to God whoever he first sees upon his return. Storgè fears that nothing but doom shall come of Jephtha's promise, but Iphis reassures her. Jephtha calls the Israelites to arms, and a chorus sings of God's support. Act II begins with Hamor describing the Israelites' victory to Iphis, who prepares, with an attendant chorus of virgins, for her father's return. Zebul and Jephtha enter, singing victoriously, then Iphis enters, virgin chorus in tow. Jephtha, remembering his vow, drives his daughter away and then explains all to Zebul, Storgè, and Hamor. They urge him to spare her, but Iphis accepts her fate with grace and nobility, believing the vow to be instrumental in Israel's victory. Jephtha breaks down, torn between his honor and his love for his daughter. The chorus sings of the fleeting uncertainty of earthly peace and happiness. In Act III, Jephtha prays for intervention of the angels and Iphis sings adieu. The priests hesitate to perform the sacrifice on the grounds that it is contrary to the law of God and they, too, pray for God's intervention. An angel appears and stops the sacrifice, declaring that no vow can disannul the law of God and calling on Iphis to remain a virgin and dedicate her life to God. The angel commends Jephtha's faith. There is much rejoicing.

The biblical account of Jephtha has a radically different ending: Jephtha's daughter takes two months to grieve her virginity in the mountains, returns, and is sacrificed. By employing the ancient Greek dramatic device of *deus ex machina*, Rev. Morell ironically crafts a libretto that eschews the tradition of Greek tragedy in favor of superimposing a Christian message that recalls the story of Abraham and Isaac.[17] Jephtha is let off the hook for trying to bargain with God and Iphis seems overjoyed at her celibate future.

Dramatic failings aside, Handel's music and characterization remains masterful. Through his arias, Jephtha is fleshed out from a deceptive archetype in the opening act ("Virtue my soul shall still embrace"; "His mighty arm") to a tragic hero in Act II ("Open thy marble jaws, O tomb"). His struggles continue in an Act-III arioso ("Hide thy hated beams, O sun") until he is granted relief and reprieve in a final arioso ("For ever blessed be thy holy name"). Iphis, too, undergoes a journey from static to dramatic, with early arias and duets employing dance forms and rhythms that recall an innocent child, maturing through the second and third acts until her final subdued aria ("Farewell, ye limpid springs and floods"), which paints a portrait of a selfless yet distraught woman.

---

17 In the Book of Genesis, an angel intervenes to prevent Abraham from sacrificing his son, Isaac, to God.

The chorus largely plays the role of the Israelites, functioning much like a Greek chorus, serving as commentators on rather than participants in the action. Eleven of the 24 arias are in *da capo* form, with *Jephtha* maintaining a fine balance between drama and reflection.

Oratorio Legacy

Just as Handel's operas went out of fashion and returned, so, too, did his oratorios. For a time considered unwieldly and bulky, the lack of staging and off-putting contrivances of plot have over the years been sublimated by the strength of Handel's music and powerful characterizations. While a glance through the current catalog shows available *Messiah* recordings far outnumbering Handel's second-place oratorio (*Saul*) sevenfold, others hold a presence: in addition to *Saul*, the most popular recordings currently available appear to be *Israel in Egypt, Judas Maccabeus, Solomon,* and *Theodora.* (And recordings of the oratorios—even excluding *Messiah*— outpace those of Handel's operas by nearly half.) Looking for a pattern within the oratorio recordings, we discover that Handel had a great run with *Saul* (1738), *Israel in Egypt* (1739) and *Messiah* (1742), which coincides, not coincidentally, with the start of Handel's first period of maturity vis-à-vis the English oratorio (1738–1745) noted above, wherein oratorio would ultimately replace opera as Handel's form of choice. *Judas Maccabeus* (1747) is the strongest of Handel's "occasional" oratorios, while *Solomon* (1749) and *Theodora* (1750) find a composer in his winter years who has mastered his form and whose music has veered away from the dramatic and toward reflection. The positioning of *Messiah* within Handel's first period of oratorio maturity in combination with the limitation of a nondramatic libretto that encouraged Handel to presage—for a few weeks—the reflective maturity of his later years lends more weather to the notion, stated in the Introduction, of *Messiah* as Handel's perfect storm.

Chapter 3

ᗧ essiah *Libretto*

THOUGH HANDEL TRADITIONALLY TOOK more
of a collaborative role in oratorios with librettist Charles
Jennens, no such collaboration took place with the libretto
for *Messiah*. This is likely because the text for *Messiah* is
an assemblage of short selections of biblical text—taken
primarily from the 1611 Authorized King James Version
and also from the Book of Common Prayer (for passages
from *Psalms*)—and it was left to Jennens, a devout member
of the Church of England, to assemble the texts without
editorial suggestion or interference from Handel. It should
be noted that Handel regularly sought out Jennens' musical critique for drafts of *Messiah* before the 1742 Dublin
premiere, and that the librettist in fact attempted a keyboard reduction score of *Messiah*, likely with the intention
of playing through the work to test Handel's settings. If
Jennens was at times difficult and demanding of Handel,
he remained a lifelong admirer of the composer and kept

a personal library of Handel manuscripts which still serves Handel scholars today.[18]

Jennens' setting of *Messiah* was doubtless influenced by the unspoken prohibition against the representation of Jesus Christ on stage that had held sway in England since the late 1500s. This is perhaps why the librettist compiled his oratorio primarily out of Old Testament prophecy, using Gospel narrative only for the annunciation to the shepherds and casting Christ's words always in the third person. As with Handel, the restrictions placed on Jennens helped to produce a final opus that was likely stronger than had he had carte blanche to write a libretto for *Jesus, The Musical.*

The libretto for *Messiah* is organized into a traditional three-act operatic and oratorio form. Part One concerns prophecies of the Savior and their fulfillment in his incarnation. Part Two journeys from Christ's passion to his second coming. Part Three deals with Christ as Savior. Jennens' 1743 wordbook gives *Messiah* an operatic treatment, further dividing the acts into scenes:

Part One: (I) The prophecy of Salvation: the Gospel, "good news"; (II) The judgment that will accompany the appearance of the Savior; (III) The prophecy of the Virgin Birth; (IV) The Incarnation announced to the Shepherds; (V) The Savior's redemptive and healing miracles.

Part Two: (I) Christ's passion, scourging and crucifixion; (II) Christ's death, passage through Hell and Resurrection; (III) Christ's Ascension; (IV) Christ's Reception in Heaven;

---

[18] The autographs for more than eighty percent of Handel's output—roughly 17,000 pages—are preserved in the British Library and the Fitzwilliam Museum, Cambridge.

(V) Whitsun, the gift of tongues, the beginning of evangelism; (VI) The world's rejection of the Gospel; (VII) God's triumph.

Part Three: (I) The promise of eternal life and triumph over Original Sin; (II) The Day of Judgment and general Resurrection; (III) Victory over death and sin; (IV) Acclamation of the Messiah.

Messiah is a work without dramatic action, due largely to Jennens' unornamented libretto, comprising Scripture selections that philosophically relate the Christian belief in the birth, death, and resurrection of Jesus Christ rather than dramatic events from the life of Christ. Weaving texts from the Old and the New Testaments—*Isaiah, Malachi, Luke, Zechariah, Matthew, John, Psalms, Lamentations, Hebrews, Romans, Revelation, Job* and *Corinthians*—Jennens constructs a Christian narrative that succeeds without characters and narrative action. But *Messiah* remains a drama, one in which the momentum is internal and intellectual rather than external and visceral. Knowledge of the historical biblical narrative is assumed, permitting, in rather avant-garde fashion, a commentary and meditation on events not explicitly presented.

Credit is due to Jennens beyond that of an "assembler" of Scripture. Rarely did he make considerable changes to the original Scripture he chose for *Messiah*, but the changes he did make were subtle and effective. He frequently omitted repeated verbs as well as conjunctions ("[and] the crooked [shall be made] straight") in order to make the Scripture as pithy as possible. In addition, the librettist occasionally substituted pronouns and verb tenses ("He *was* despised" for "He *is* despised") in order to better unify or dramatize the text or improve the ease of singing and comprehension. On rare occasion Jennens would reword text ("O thou that tellest good tidings to Zion" for "O Zion, that bringest good tidings"), always to the betterment of narrative flow.

Finally, it is worth noting that for Jennens, a traditionalist Christian, *Messiah* represented an opportunity to reassert traditional Christian values, particularly in the rising movement of Deism, a religious philosophy that derives the existence and nature of God from reason and personal experience and rejects supernatural events—including miracles and prophecy. Jennens, through his focus on Redemption, effectively returns attention to Christianity's principal tenet. And while the historical role of evangelism in Christianity is tainted at best, to label Jennens' zeal for his work as anti-Deist or anti-Semitic, rather than simply pro-Christian, seems grossly unwarranted.[19] Standing in direct contradiction to charges of the work's anti-Semitism is the rich charitable tradition that *Messiah* sparked and continues to uphold, to Christians and non-Christians alike—in a true Christian spirit.

Jennens marked his libretto with the inscription *Majora canamus* (Let us sing of great things) and summed up the message of *Messiah* in a scriptural epigraph:

> And without controversy, great is the mystery of Godliness: God was manifested in the flesh, justified by the spirit, seen of angels, preached among the gentiles,

---

19 Cf. Michael Marissen. "Unsettling History of That Joyous 'Hallelujah,'" *New York Times.* April 8, 2007. Cf. James Oestreich. "Hallelujah Indeed: Debating Handel's Anti-Semitism", *New York Times.* April 23, 2007. Cf. Wendy Heller. "Wendy Heller on Handel's 'Messiah,'" *New York Times.* April 23, 2007. Cf. Ruth Smith. "Ruth Smith on Handel's 'Messiah,'" *New York Times.* April 25, 2007.

believed on in the world, received up in glory. (I Timothy 3.16)

In whom are hid all the treasures of wisdom and knowledge. (Colossians 2.3)

essiah *Revisions*

IT IS DIFFICULT TO LOCATE a definitive version of Handel's *Messiah* because, in the words of music writer Michael Steinberg, "*Messiah* is a moving target." We know that the work was composed by Handel at a feverish pace in 24 days in the summer of 1741, and that he adapted and changed the work every time he performed it, including the first performance, until 1753. These changes were often practical, with transpositions of music and reallocations of movements made based on what singers and musicians were available for the performances in question. Certainly many changes and revisions of the Handel-directed performances of *Messiah* (1742–1759) came at the behest of soloists who wanted their arias expressly suited to their voices. The Dublin performance in 1742 was a rough-and-ready affair of a rather small ensemble. Handel had taken only two sopranos and an alto with him to Dublin and likely had to scrounge for local talent to fill out the vocalist roster; Handel ultimately ended up substituting three arias with recitative. He was also without oboists but was likely more concerned with larger issues of performance and audience reception.

Correspondence from Charles Jennens to Handel shows that Jennens sought revision from Handel as early as 1743, asking him to "retouch the weak parts." For the 1743 performances, Handel included a setting of the text "Their sound is gone out" at Jennens' insistence along with other additions to adapt the score to the current roster of soloists, including the substitution of a soprano for an alto soloist in the duet and chorus version of "How beautiful are the feet."[20] Jennens continued to assail Handel for further revisions in 1744 despite the composer's battle with illness. The friendship between the two became strained until it was reconciled by the death of James Miller, Handel's librettist for *Joseph and His Brethren*, which sent the composer seeking Jennens' good graces in the hopes that he would write future libretti. Handel himself took the initiative, writing to Jennens in 1744: "Be pleased to point out those passages in the *Messiah* which You think require altering." So it was the 1745 revival that contained the most revision at the request of Jennens. The librettist found Handel's 1743 aria "Their sound is gone out" too innocuous to earn the reaction for the movement that followed, "Why do the nations?" Therefore Handel wrote a chorus and restored the original aria version of "How beautiful are the feet" to precede it. Further, Handel recast "Rejoice greatly" in common time to better balance out the numerous compound-meter settings of Part One.

The year 1749 saw important revisions by Handel that became "standard," including the best-known "Rejoice greatly" in 4/4 time and the choral arrangement of "Their sound is gone out." The 1749 version of *Messiah* is also notable for

---

20 See Appendix—*Messiah* Structure.

Handel's *ripieno* directions, a term used to distinguish when all orchestral players should be used. *Con ripieno* indicates that all desks of players should play, while *senza repieni* calls for only the first desks. From Handel's use of these markings, we can infer that the 1749 version employed a larger string section than was typically used; Handel's instructions here, however, were not meant to be applied in perpetuity, but were made—as per his practical shifts in vocal parts—to adapt to circumstances of the performance. Of special significance is a 1749 concert that took place at the Foundling Hospital, which saw the premiere of Handel's "Foundling Hospital Anthem," *Blessed are they that considereth the Poor and Needy*, assembled from movements borrowed from earlier works as well as *Messiah's* "Hallelujah" chorus. It is perhaps here where royalty (the Prince and Princess of Wales) first stood for "Hallelujah" and began the tradition; it is doubtful that such a practice was set in motion by King George II at the 1743 London performance, as is popularly believed, since his presence at the performance has not been verified by press or diarists.

The year 1750 marked Handel's final significant revisions to the score, inspired by new soloists that included renowned Italian castrato Gaetano Guadagni. Handel composed two new settings for castrato of arias formerly assigned to bass and soprano: "But who may abide?" and "Thou art gone up on high." "How beautiful are the feet" was also set for alto. With Guadagni in Ireland in 1752, Handel used two different casts, which resulted in two different performing versions. The version performed at Covent Garden in March of 1752 calls for a solo quartet of soprano, contralto, tenor, and bass. This production is closest to the standard Victorian sequence of the Ebenezer Prout 1902 edition and so came to be the version that "authentic" *Messiahs* attempt to re-create. The Covent Garden performance assigned the Guadagni versions of "But who may abide?" and "Thou art gone up on high" to alto and employed a revised soprano arrangement of "How beautiful are the feet." The 1752 version also employs the short version of "Why do the nations?" Even after he became blind in 1754, there is evidence to suggest that Handel still officially oversaw performances of *Messiah* at the Foundling Hospital. His death in 1759 came between the *Messiah* performance that closed the theatre season on April 6 and the Foundling Hospital performance on May 3. Performances between 1753 and his death appear to have changed very little, so it is likely that the 1754 score presented to the Hospital upon Handel's death incorporates the vast majority of the composer's myriad changes. Still, neither the 1754 nor any particular version of *Messiah* bears the title of the "official" or "authentic" version.

During Handel's lifetime, performances of *Messiah* were given in Dublin and throughout England under auspices other than the Foundling Hospital—to which Handel made no objection. It is likely that the various performances, though authorized, used different versions of the score. In any case, continuity was preserved to the posthumous performances of *Messiah* in London, which continued at Covent Garden Theatre until 1774 and Foundling Hospital until 1768. A full score of *Messiah* was published in 1767, eliminating any difficulty of access. In 1771, the Foundling Hospital performances began to bulk up on choristers, increasing their ranks from 30 to 56, outnumbering orchestral players.

These numbers steadily increased. In 1784 at Westminster Abbey, the musicians and choristers multiplied to encompass a total fighting force of 500, numbers that set the tone for the 1800s, which favored an aesthetic that provided a larger orchestral and choral sound. This was compounded by the rise of musical education among the masses and easy access to cheap vocal scores for all. Often instruments were added to performances (additional accompaniment) without scoring alterations, but at times, in order to adapt *Messiah* to the then current "classical" orchestra, additional wind parts were written (strengthening accompaniment) which may have been at odds with Handel's musical style and taste.[21]

Given Handel's propensity for adapting and arranging in order to keep his music fresh and accessible to his audience, it was certainly in keeping with Handelian principle that Mozart arranged *Messiah* in 1789, with his publishers offering the explanation on the title page of Mozart's 1802 edition: "Händel's *Messiah* / Arranged for Greater Serviceablility for Our Day / By W. A. Mozart." The Mozart arrangement is tasteful, dark, and beautiful—in short, Mozartean. The change most evident to the ear is the shift from English to German to appease the Viennese. While generally preserving Handel's vocal lines and string parts, Mozart strengthens a good deal of the orchestration, adding parts for flutes, oboes, clarinets, bassoons, horns, trombones, trumpets, and timpani. This, as much as anything makes Mozart's *Messiah*

---

21 A distinction can be made here: "additional" accompaniments kept with the balance of Handel's score, while "strengthening" necessitated compositional change, through scoring or additional harmony. Handel himself strengthened *Messiah* through the addition of oboes and bassoons in 1745.

decidedly un-Handelian, as part of Handel's genius is how he does more with less than most. Mozart also reassigned and reorchestrated many of the arias, and made some cuts (most of them unfortunate). Throughout the 1800s, it was commonplace to cut "Thou art gone up on high," the B section of "The trumpet shall sound" and the music that followed through "Worthy is the Lamb," cuts which had no precedence in Handel's revision, and are frankly indefensible from both musical and dramatic perspectives.

Published in 1803, "Mozart's Messiah" included elements from an arrangement by Johann Adam Hillier, which opened the door to other arrangements, including Robert Franz's "completion" of Mozart's score (1885), and Ebenezer Prout's 1902 edition with "additional accompaniments." The spread of musical literacy in the 1800s and the formation of an amateur choral society in London in 1833 had cemented the popularity of Messiah for the years to come, but it also led to the rise of unwieldy choruses and massive orchestras. The bigger-is-better mandate became all too much for critic George Bernard Shaw, who, in his review of an 1891 festival performance, cried out for a "thoroughly rehearsed and exhaustively studied performance of Messiah" with "twenty capable artists." His 1891 review was 75 years ahead of its time for its prescience into the rise in popularity of historically informed performance in the latter half of the twentieth century. The 1950s saw a renewed interest in Handel scholarship, with John Tobin conducting the London Choral Society in a performance of Messiah that attempted to restore Handel's original scoring (albeit on a larger scale) and performance practices. More recently, professional "Baroque" orchestras, equipped with period instruments, have done their best to counteract the bloated practices of the nineteenth century.

Of the numerous editions of *Messiah*, the three principal performing editions in use today are the Peters Edition, ed. Donald Burrows; Novello Edition, ed. Watkins Shaw; and the Bärenreiter Edition, ed. John Tobin.

Chapter 5

ℳessiah *Analysis*

THIS ANALYSIS OF HANDEL'S *MESSIAH* uses the 1750 version of the score (conducted by the composer), preferred not only for its transparency and spare orchestration, but for its incorporation of the last revisions that Handel made for aesthetic reasons rather than solely practical concerns. Voicings, soloists,[22] orchestration and text of *Messiah* vary depending on the version and recording.

Part One

1. "Sinfony" [overture]

Handel's overture to *Messiah* is a French overture, a form which originated in the mid-1600s at the court of Louis XIV. Since one of its purposes was to signal the entrance of the king to the opera, the form is naturally infused with an element of fanfare, retained here in Handel's slow and stately opening

---

22 Countertenor arias in the 1750 version are generally written as soprano arias in other versions of *Messiah*.

strains, its solemn, skipping rhythm (a French trait) easily calling to mind a royal procession. But this overture, quite plain in its orchestration, holds some menace and despair in its dark and unornamented opening (in E minor), perhaps indicating that all is not right with the world. From out of this darkness, hope, in the form of a bright fugue, emerges. Here the fugal subject is introduced by the first violin and first oboe and then imitated by the remaining voices in succession (save the violas): first the second violin and second oboe together, then the basses. Though the Overture's elegant fugue is more buoyant than its *Grave* opening, Handel makes a point of not modulating into a major key once again, asserting that trials and tribulations lie ahead.

2. Tenor recitative

> *Comfort ye, comfort ye my people, saith your God. Speak ye comfortably to Jerusalem, and cry unto her, That her warfare is accomplished, That her iniquity is pardoned.*
>
> *The voice of him that crieth in the wilderness, Prepare ye the way of the Lord, Make straight in the desert a highway for our God. (Isaiah 40.1–3)* [23]

Nos. 2–4 comprise the "good news" section of *Messiah*.[24] The uncertainty of the opening minor key is broken by the surprising light of E major in a gentle and pastoral *ritornello*, which here is the orchestral motive at the very opening of the recitative in the strings that returns throughout in various appearances. In addition to the repetition of the *ritornello*, the tenor's repetition of "comfort ye" is, in itself, comforting.

---

23 Alterations of biblical text per Jennens' libretto; capitalization, spelling and punctuation of same per Zondervan's *King James Version Study Bible*.

24 Part One (I) as defined in the Libretto chapter (or see APPENDIX).

Handel also makes the tenor as comfortable as possible, giving him space when needed (cutting out all instruments for a solo "ye") and elsewhere supporting with a cushion of strings that mirrors the text. Handel reflects the tenor's text musically, writing strong motives for the repetition of "saith your God," applying harmonic tension in "iniquity," and resolving it with "is pardoned." Handel sharply shifts from accompanied recitative to a *secco* recitative style ("dry" or unaccompanied) when the tenor reaches the exclamatory text beginning, "The voice of him that crieth in the wilderness . . ." In doing so, Handel permits the beauty of the text's parallel structure (wilderness/desert; prepare/make straight; the way/a highway) to shine unadorned, and, on a more practical level, he creates a makeshift introduction to the first aria.

3. Tenor aria

> *Every valley shall be exalted, And every mountain and hill made low, The crooked straight, And the rough places plain.*
> *(Isaiah 40.4)*

This aria stands as one of the most glorious clinics of text painting in all of classical music. Handel mimics the contours of the land of which the tenor sings: the soloist climbs into (descending) "valley" and out of it (ascending). "Mountain" makes a great peak, while "hill" receives a smaller one. "Low" is given a low note. For the text "the crooked straight," "crooked" is given three or four syllables on different pitches, while "straight" is one straight tone. "Rough" is roughly trilled, while "plain" is given an extended, sweeping setting, evoking a wide expanse of space, remaining constant in pitch or gently rising or falling to a new elevation. Handel's treatment of "exalted" literally exalts the word, giving it delightful *coloratura*, elaborate and florid ornamentation. Though the orchestration frames the aria, its material is centrally focused on the musical lines of the voice, presaging, echoing and affirming—familiarizing the listener with the tenor's lines before he even hears them and then recalling them afterward in a tightly constructed form with modest means of strings and continuo. Not to be missed is the variable five-note motive (sometimes with a pickup note) of the *basso continuo* that delightedly introduces the instrumental phrases (it is the first five notes of the aria) and responds to, or closes, the tenor's declamations—with a playful wink.

4. Chorus

> And the glory of the Lord shall be revealed, And all flesh shall see it together: For the mouth of the Lord hath spoken it. (Isaiah 40.5)

The chorus's message here is simple, as is the logic that frames it. Handel matches both in his graceful and seemingly simplistic setting. Four musical motives make up the material. First, the altos introduce "And the glory, the glory of the Lord"; then, the tenors sing: "shall be revealed." These two musical shapes intertwine and cadence, and then give way to the introduction of the third (altos: "and all flesh shall see it together") and the fourth, a chant-like motive that enters stealthily on a fixed tone from the men: "for the mouth of the Lord has spoken it." These two motives combine and then all four are brought together in the finale, creating a sense of comfort and completion. This chorus is in 3/4, but the rhythm is felt in one, with Handel assuring that the naturally strong first beat is emphasized through placement of the chorus's text and cadences of the strings on same, which creates a rocking easiness that governs until the closing "hath spoken it," which is given an "Amen" treatment, impressing that the words are the Lord's words.

5. Bass recitative

> *Thus saith the Lord of hosts; Yet once, a little while, And I will shake the heavens and the earth, the sea and the dry land; And I will shake all nations, and the desire of all nations shall come. (Haggai 2.6–7)*
>
> *The Lord, whom ye seek, shall suddenly come to his temple, Even the messenger of the covenant, whom ye delight in: Behold, he shall come, saith the Lord of hosts. (Malachi 3.1)*

Nos. 5–7 comprise the "judgment" section of *Messiah* (Part One, (II)). Aggressive syncopated rhythms in the strings introduce the bass soloist, who takes the rhythm on himself in his announcement: "Thus saith the Lord . . ." Handel illuminates the verb "shake" to dramatic effect, giving the bass an inhuman run of through-composed sixteenth notes the first three times the word appears. The strings strike in emphasis during "shake" and then excitedly take up the bass's sixteenth notes in sympathetic reverberation as the bass details the effect of the shaking. The treatment is later carried from the word "shake" to "desire." The *Malachi* portion of the recitative returns to *secco* recitative, but maintains the syncopated rhythms of the opening. Throughout the recitative, the rhythm of the strings is in unison, enhancing the "earthquake" effect of shock and awe.

6. Countertenor aria

> *But who may abide the day of his coming? And who shall stand when he appeareth? For he is like a refiner's fire. (Malachi 3.1)*

This aria is divided into sharply distinct and contrasting sections. In the first, rhetorical questions are poignantly posed in a gently lilting *Larghetto* 3/8 in a lovely duet with *basso continuo*. The second section, in common time, reveals why the questions are unanswerable. *Prestissimo* strings underscore nimble but forceful *coloratura* that surround the "refiner's fire." Then, the questions are posed again (in 3/8), followed by the scorching common-time strings, who close with a fiery coda.

7. Chorus

> *And he shall purify the sons of Levi, That they may offer*
> *unto the Lord an offering in righteousness. (Malachi 3.3)*

Just as the purification of the Levites[25] is the climax of *Malachi*, so, too, is it the climax of this sequence of *Messiah* (5–7). The sixteenth-note *coloratura* from the previous aria is continued, but cast in a calmer atmosphere; the terror of the "refiner's fire," gives way to the serene, less violent imagery of purification. In a humble and spare texture, the sopranos introduce the first motive, with ornamented treatment of "purify" achieving a satisfying delayed rhyme with "Levi".[26] which enhances the perceived justness of the text. The text setting is further aided by the *basso continuo*, always an interesting (and signifying) element to follow in Baroque music and in Handel especially. Here the *continuo* is responsible for building the excitement of the chorus, which it does by not dwelling on its cadences but by shape-shifting throughout in

---

25 The Hebrew priesthood

26 Fans of Steely Dan will already be familiar with the technique of the late-arriving rhyme (e.g., "Biscayne Bay/Where the Cuban gentlemen sleep all day"). That Handel employed such a cadence over two centuries previous is an avant-garde masterstroke.

running eighth notes from the opening pickup that precedes the entrance of the chorus. The voices build up gradually in the chorus: though Handel hints at a fugue, voices drop out after stating the subject, so that the setting is in duet form for the opening phrases, then in three parts until the four-part harmony in unison rhythm: "That they may offer . . . in righteousness."

8. Alto recitative

> Behold, a Virgin shall conceive, and bear a Son, and shall call his name Emmanuel. God with us. (Isaiah 7.14; Matthew 1.23)

Nos. 8–12 comprise the Virgin Birth prophecy section of *Messiah* (Part One, (III)). Leaving G minor for D major, Handel's setting of this brief recitative shines with a simplicity that recalls an older style: this morsel, an understated promise of the prophet, would be quite at home in Carissimi's *Jephte*.

9. Alto aria and chorus

> O thou that tellest good tidings to Zion, get thee up into the high mountain; O thou that tellest good tidings to Jerusalem, lift up thy voice with strength; Lift it up, be not afraid; Say unto the cities of Judah, Behold your God. (Isaiah 40.9)
> O thou that tellest good tidings to Zion, Arise, shine; for thy light is come, And the glory of the Lord is risen upon thee. (Isaiah 60.1)

The alto aria and following chorus are strictly linked, both textually and musically, with the chorus affirming the words of the soloist with a populist urgency. The music accompanying these "good tidings" is kept light thanks to a bouncing 6/8 meter and joyful noodling in the violins. A touch of text painting helps keep the feeling of naturalism and optimism: the contours of the alto's second "mountain" are illustrated; subsequent leaps upward for the soloist's "lift up/thy voice/ with strength/be not afraid" lift the spirit with it; exalting *coloratura* for "Arise" mirrors the motion; and the glorifica-tion of "glory" (a word which is given extended *coloratura* and ornamentation) drives the point home. The chorus's text is unadorned by comparison to that of the alto, with an emphasis on message—the same matter with less art.

10. Bass recitative

> For behold, darkness shall cover the earth, And gross darkness the people: But the Lord shall arise upon thee, and his glory shall be seen upon thee, And the Gentiles shall come to thy light, And kings to the brightness of thy rising. (Isaiah 60.2–3)

In contrast with the brightness of the previous aria and chorus, "darkness" is the subject matter of this recitative. Handel evokes the darkness through ponderous strings and their foreboding figures set atop a bass-line *ostinato* (repeated figure). In a contrasting section, light breaks through in a major key with the text: "But the Lord shall arise." Handel also shifts the string accompaniment in this section from six-teenth notes to eighth notes, dissipating anxiety with a calmer and sturdier base to support to the bass's reassuring words. "Arise" climbs through the bass register, falling in gentle denouement on "glory."

11. Bass aria

> The people that walked in darkness have seen a great light: And they that dwell in the land of the shadow of death, upon them hath the light shined. (Isaiah 9.2)

The bass aria picks up on the "darkness" string motive from the connected recitative as the text again returns from brightness to darkness. The halting tempo evokes walking in the dark and the music itself seems to grope about, searching (chromatically) for a toehold. Handel uses the parallel structure of the text to guide his musical plan: darkness and light are twice contrasted, permitting the composer to divide his text into two dark–light sections. Darkness is in a minor key, with light in a major. Handel effects a contrast by setting the "dark" section in a unison monody (and rhythm) with the strings and bass soloist; the strings open into a richer fuller harmony for the arrival of the light (when the bass reaches "great light"). Yet the darkness is not ultimately penetrated, as the aria ends with darkness holding sway in a minor key, setting up the wondrous brightness of the chorus to follow.

12. Chorus

> For unto us a child is born, unto us a Son is given: and the government shall be upon his shoulder: And his name shall be called Wonderful, Counsellor, The mighty God, The everlasting Father, The Prince of Peace. (Isaiah 9.6)

Arguably the greatest chorus of Messiah, "For unto us a child is born" is pristine in its elegance, simplicity, and mastery of form. It transcends time, sounding both ancient and prescient. While Handel has previously taken pains to emphasize the meter, here the common-time bar lines are intentionally blurred, with staggered entrances designed to extend musical phrases to infinity. The material is laid out simply, with the opening text in the soprano given a climbing coloratura on "born" that is also taken as an obbligato (an essential instrumental part, secondary in importance only to the melody) in the strings. The tenor then introduces a second section, "And the government . . .," which is imitated in the soprano, followed by the alto and bass together. All vocal parts unfold and swell to the climax of "Wonderful . . .," where Handel, in a stroke of genius, gives each noun or noun phrase space to breathe, with the strings supporting the musical line in a purposeful climbing sixteenth-note figuration that conjures imagery of unbroken lines and unblemished beauty. This is a wondrous moment of choral unity that Handel has judiciously saved for the occasion of announcing the birth of the Messiah. This celebratory outpouring brings to a close the prophecy of the Virgin Birth.

13. Pifa [pastoral symphony]

Numbers 13–17 comprise the Incarnation announced to the Shepherds (Part One, (IV)). This instrumental interlude, modestly orchestrated for three violins, viola and bass, evokes shepherds at their flocks through the use of musical devices traditionally associated with pastoral imagery: pedal point (a sustained note under harmonic movement); and rhythms and phrasing common to a *Siciliana*,[27] a traditionally pastoral and rustic instrumental movement—mastered by Handel early in his career—that resembles a slow *Gigue*. The interlude permits a respite, a shift in energy, and prepares the soprano recitative to follow.

14, 15, 16. Soprano recitatives

There were shepherds abiding in the field, keeping watch over their flock by night.

---

27 A Siciliana is thought to be the basis for the Christmas carol *Stille Nacht* ("Silent Night").

> *And lo, the angel of the Lord came upon them and the glory of the Lord shone round about them: and they were sore afraid. (Luke 2.8–2.9)*
>
> *And the angel said unto them, Fear not: for behold, I bring you good tidings of great joy, which shall be to all people. For unto you is born this day, in the city of David, a Saviour, which is Christ the Lord. (Luke 2.10–2.11)*
>
> *And suddenly there was with the angel a multitude of the heavenly host, praising God, and saying, (Luke 2.13)*

Handel alternates the treatment of the soprano's recitative text: *secco/accompagnato/secco/accompagnato*. It is the arrival of the angels (Luke 2.9 and 2.13) that are given the accompaniment—the violins' broken chords evoking the flutter of wings[28]—while the angels' holy dialogue (delivered again in antiquated Carissimi style) is unadorned. The primary function of these recitatives, however, is to set up the chorus for a glorious entrance, doubly confirmed by the fact that the recitative text ends with "praising God, and saying . . . ."

17. Chorus

> *Glory to God in the highest, And peace on earth, Good will towards men. (Luke 2.14)*

Breaking with the pattern of recitative/aria, the sudden explosion of "Glory to God" by the chorus—with the first introduction of trumpets—after the largely spare recitative is an effective contrast. The chorus imbues the brief text with a good deal of personality. "Glory to God" is declarative; after a pause, "and peace on earth" is delivered by the men in a quiet unison, as though striving toward the condition they are describing; when "good will towards men" arrives,

---

28 Or at least a flurry of activity.

it comes with a brief fugal flirtation as the vocal parts enter in staggered imitation, as though delivering individual blessings that multiply as they are passed forward. The entire text repeats and then an instrumental coda fades away, indicating that the angels have departed and a change of scene is forthcoming.

18. Soprano aria

> *Rejoice greatly, O daughter of Zion; Shout, O daughter of Jerusalem, Behold, thy King cometh unto thee; He is the righteous Saviour, and he shall speak peace unto the heathen. (Zechariah 9.9–9.10)*

Nos. 18–21 comprise the miracles of the Savior (Part One, (V)). The aria that opens the sequence is laid out in an A–B–A form. Written in common time but felt in a danceable two beats per measure, the opening "rejoice greatly" is given nimble sixteenth-note *coloratura* which lends this aria a light exuberance. The strings mimic the soprano's line, sharing her mood. But when the soprano reaches "He is the righteous Saviour," Handel slows and sobers the pace: the music in the B–section is no longer in a dance form and the length of the measures is doubled: the music is felt in a calm four. The singer delivers Zechariah's words on the Savior tenderly in a near recitative. But Handel ultimately returns to the joyous opening, adding a triplet feel in the recapitulation of the A–section for variety. The strings close the aria with a royal skipping rhythm—recalling the tone of the Overture.

19. Alto recitative

> *Then shall the eyes of the blind be opened, And the ears of the deaf unstopped. Then shall the lame man leap as a hart, and the tongue of the dumb shall sing. (Isaiah 35.5–6)*

This brief recitative stresses the linking of spiritual and physical healing and gives signs that the Messianic age is at hand. The alto establishes a context for her aria, which will deliver Christ's words: "Come unto me, all ye that labour and are heavy laden . . ." (altered by Jennens to the third person).

20. Alto/countertenor aria

> He shall feed his flock like a shepherd: And he shall gather the lambs with his arm, And carry them in his bosom, And gently lead those that are with young. Come unto him all ye that labour, come unto him that are heavy laden, and he will give you rest. Take his yoke upon you, and learn of him, for he is meek and lowly of heart, and ye shall find rest unto your souls. (Isaiah 40.11; Matthew 11.28–29)

This text concerning flocks, shepherds, and lambs begs for pastoral treatment, and Handel obliges, using F major (a traditional pastoral key) and employing the aforementioned form of the *Siciliana*. A gentle flow and simple harmonic progression is characteristic of the form and of this aria, too, which is written in 12/8 and rocks gently back and forth in a soothing rhythm, channeling Christ's compassion. The strings are richly supportive throughout, cradling the soloist. Handel avoids monotony by not only dividing the aria between two soloists but by varying the outcomes of phrases (note the different treatments of "with his arm") and by adding contrast, such as the unexpected minor that follows "He will give you rest."

21. Chorus

> His yoke is easy, his burden is light. (Matthew 11.30)

A direct continuation of the text of Matthew following the aria, this chorus is speedy and light, complementing the text:

"His yoke is easy."[29] In fact, it is the "easy" of this text that is stressed (and given *coloratura* in the style of the "Rejoice" aria),[30] not the presence of the yoke or the burden. Handel adds to the light feel by marshalling the chorus in duets until nearly the end of the piece, when all four voice parts sing their text in unison, but without fanfare, bringing Part One to a modest, gentle close.

Part Two

22. Chorus

Behold the Lamb of God, that taketh away the sin of the world. (John 1.29)

Nos. 22–30 comprise Christ's passion, scourging, and crucifixion (Part Two, (I)). Here *Messiah* shifts from the promise of the coming in Part One to redemption through Christ's suffering. As throughout the libretto, the text in Part Two focuses on reflection rather than description. A traditional recounting of the Passion is eschewed in favor of focusing on its redemptive power. This piece, like the aria "He shall feed his flock" (No. 20), has pastoral imagery, but here the burden is not light, the yoke not easy. In a slow syncopated (dotted rhythm) unfolding, we feel the weight and pathos of the Lamb of God. The setting is dominated by the dotted rhythm, a device used consistently by both Handel and Bach when depicting passionate expression. The skipping rhythm

---

29 Cf. No. 7. Handel employs the same *basso continuo* pickup that opened the chorus "And he shall purify." The effect in the major key ("His yoke is easy") is similar, but lacks the urgency of this previous chorus, evoked there by the use of the minor key.

30 Cf. No. 18.

possesses an innate nobility (recall *Messiah's* overture) yet is also innately fragile, with the syncopation lending the music an agonizing delay and a pathetic stutter—as though the leaps in rhythm require a leap in faith from one note to the next. The oboes help to darken the palette, notably when they play in unison with the sopranos on a monodic solo "that taketh"—as the other voices are gently added—stretching the B-flat piteously through the phrase until a reassuring major key takes control, if only for a moment. Lugubrious G minor holds sway at the finale.

23. Alto aria

> *He was despised and rejected of men; A man of sorrows, and acquainted with grief. (Isaiah 53.3)*
>
> *He gave his back to the smiters, and his cheeks to them that plucked off the hair: he hid not his face from shame and spitting. (Isaiah 50.6)*

This celebrated alto aria is in A–B–A form, with the "smiters" text (Isaiah 50.6) making up the agitated B–section, bookended by the more tranquil declaration of the Messiah's despised condition. The first point of interest is Handel's phrasing, which creates a dialogue between the alto and the orchestra (previewed in the opening *ritornello*, a dialogue among the strings) by breaking the alto's melody into short phrases, interspersed with replies from the orchestra, e.g. "He was despised . . . despised and rejected . . . rejected of men." It is as though the alto can hardly bear to tell the story, interspersed with sobs as she catches her breath to continue. In addition, the aria is marked with a "sigh motif" in the strings in the introductory *ritornello* and the interlude that adds to the piteous quality of the music. The middle section, which is a near *arioso*, is distinguished by a violent accompaniment in the strings (in a dotted rhythm)[31] that matches the horror being described.[32]

24. Chorus

> *Surely he hath borne our griefs, And carried our sorrows;*
> *he was wounded for our transgressions, He was bruised for*
> *our iniquities; The chastisement of our peace was upon him.*
> *(Isaiah 53.4–5)*

The dotted rhythms[33] from the opening chorus and preceding aria are present here for the first of three choruses, a declamatory *parlando* (a style of singing that approximates speech) that feels cold and matter-of-fact as compared to "He was despised." The two main motives of this chorus are "Surely he" and "The chastisement", which effects a fine contrast. The text setting, however, borders on the ridiculous, With "Surely he" making for an awkward motive and "he hath" being spat out in a pair of sixteenth notes by the hapless chorus. These two motives are separated by a slow section dealing with "transgressions" and "iniquities," and Handel surprises with the entrance of the new (and presciently Mozartean) "chastisement" motive set atop the previous (dotted-rhythm) accompaniment.

25. Chorus

> *And with his stripes we are healed. (Isaiah 53.5)*

In setting this short statement as a fugue, Handel reminds the listener that This Is The Point. He sets it well, using the

---

31 Cf. No. 22.

32 The conclusion of the B–section ends with the unaccompanied setting of "from shame and spitting," text (notably the verb) that invites an evocative *parlando*.

33 Cf. Nos. 22 and 23.

unusual and striking interval of a falling seventh in the first half of the subject ("his stripes"), and fast-moving quarter notes in the second half, ensuring that the former will catch the ear when it comes around and the latter will ensure a flowing movement and avoid aural stagnation.

26. Chorus

All we like sheep have gone astray; We have turned every one to his own way; And the Lord hath laid on him the iniquity of us all. (Isaiah 53.6)

This chorus is a fine complement to "For unto us a child is born," likely because Handel pulled from the same chamber duet composed shortly before *Messiah* for starting material for both. The motives achieve the clean quality of "For unto us . . ." and pop well against the scampering bass line. The wandering sheep are evoked by the fugal subject springing from voice to voice, with no semblance of unity. At first blush, it appears incongruous that the text "All we like sheep have gone astray . . ." is set to such joyous and buoyant music, filled with *coloratura*. But Handel's plan becomes clear in an instant, when he abruptly shifts to a sobering *Adagio* and minor key for "And the Lord hath laid on him the iniquity of us all," setting the voices in unison for the first time in this chorus (upon the arrival of the direct object of the phrase) and reminding us of the burden laid onto the Messiah and of our focus: Redemption.

27. Tenor recitative

All they that see him, laugh him to scorn: They shoot out their lips, and shake their heads, saying: (Psalms 22.7)

The dotted rhythms return with a vengeance here in order to stress the Passion and depict the crowd's scornful laughter, and the tenor exclaims the words vehemently.

28. Chorus

He trusted in God that he would deliver him: Let him deliver him, if he delight in him. (Psalms 22.8)

More venom follows as the chorus gives voice to the words that the tenor prefaced. Unlike the fugue for "And with his stripes we are healed," Handel avoids elegance here, with the chorus taking ironic pleasure in "delight" and with all vocal parts repeating bits of the subject (i.e., "would deliver him"/ "let him deliver him") again and again, creating the effect of an insensitive, spiteful crowd. Particularly (and intentionally) grating is the punched setting of "de-LIV-er," the second syllable accentuated with a high note to call attention to the motive's constant repetition.

29. Tenor recitative

Thy rebuke hath broken his heart; he is full of heaviness. He looked for some to have pity on him, but there was no man, neither found he any to comfort him. (Psalms 69.20)

Again returning to the antiquated style, this accompanied recitative differs from previous ones in that it passes through several harmonic shifts and changes of key, as the tenor's plaintive mood descends into hopelessness. Handel also has the tenor repeat much of the text, as though he is searching, in vain, for another outcome.

30. Tenor aria

Behold, and see if there be any sorrow like unto his sorrow!
(Lamentations 1.12)

The melancholic mood of the previous recitative continues
into the aria. The tenor's delivery is halting, as in the alto
aria "He was despised" (No. 23). The tenor's repetition of his
text, first for the phrase "Behold, and see," then of the entire
text, aids the mood of despondency into which the tenor
has fallen. In addition, the harmony here, unlike that of the
previous recitative, remains static, increasing the feeling that
the soloist shall remain forsaken. A closer look at the setting
reveals that every tentative rise in the tenor's line ("Behold")
is answered with a fall ("and see"). The tenor's final text,
"like unto his sorrow," returns the tenor to his lowest note—
the same on which he began the aria.

31. Soprano recitative

He was cut off out of the land of the living: For the transgres-
sions of thy people he was stricken. (Isaiah 53.8)

Nos. 31–32 comprise Christ's death, passage through Hell
and Resurrection (Part Two, (II)). This brief soprano accompanied recitative serves to reset the narrative on its focus of
Redemption, and it is also a transition between the despondency of the tenor aria that precedes it and the brightness
of the soprano aria that follows. The music shifts halfway
through from a minor key to a major one. While the shift in
color is not called for in the text, it is necessary to presage
the aria, the subject matter and change in outlook of which
latently justify the recitative's major key.

32. Soprano aria

But thou didst not leave his soul in hell; Nor didst thou suffer thy Holy One to see corruption. (Psalms 16.10)

In its strings introduction, this aria immediately and indisputably vanquishes the darkness of the minor-key settings that preceded it. It is also light and airy by design, freeing itself from earthly torments. The harmonies are simple, and are grounded by a pleasant walking bass line in the *basso continuo*. There are no contrasting sections in this aria, as Handel leans on the lightness of the music to carry the shift of mood. Gentle strings begin the aria, which the soprano imitates upon her entrance. The soprano's line is confident and plain. She reaffirms again and again "thou didst not leave"—an affirmation and also a reassurance that we are not abandoned and death is not the final word.

33. Chorus

Lift up your heads, O ye gates; And be ye lift up, ye everlasting doors; And the King of glory shall come in. Who is this King of glory? The Lord strong and mighty, The Lord mighty in battle. Lift up your heads, O ye gates; And be ye lift up, ye everlasting doors; And the King of glory shall come in! Who is the King of glory? The Lord of hosts, he is the King of glory. (Psalms 24.7–10)

No. 33 details Christ's Ascension (Part Two, (III)). If the soprano's aria established an atmosphere of confidence, the chorus raises that confidence to an expression of lofty praise and jubilation. Handel here divides his chorus in two (a double chorus), so that different groups ask and answer the question "Who is this King of glory?" The sopranos are split and altos at times sing with them (group one) and alternately with the tenors and basses (group two). Opening the chorus, the altos plus group one announce ". . . the King of glory shall come in!" Group two asks: "Who is this King of glory?" "The Lord strong and mighty . . ." replies group one and the altos. Now Handel subtly enlarges the groups. The altos join group two for the next phrase: "Lift up your heads . . ." but also join group one for the question which follows: "Who is this King of glory?" Handel has thus deceptively divided and yet increased his forces so that when all the chorus sings together for "the Lord of hosts," it comes as a climax after a buildup. For the second half of the chorus, the groups are disbanded, the sopranos reunited and the text "He is the King of glory, the Lord of hosts" is extended (notably for the *coloratura* on "glory"), staggered and repeated among solo and various combinations of vocal parts, creating the feeling of infinite space common to a song of praise—and, in the final phrase, unity of expression.

34. Tenor recitative

Unto which of the angels said he at any time, Thou art my Son, this day have I begotten thee. (Hebrew 1.5a)

Nos. 34–35 comprise Christ's Reception in Heaven (Part Two, (IV)). The tenor's brief *secco* recitative links the preceding and following chorus. It is accompanied only by *basso continuo*. The highest note falls on "day," stressing the immediacy ("this day") of the text.

35. Chorus

Let all the angels of God worship him. (Hebrew 1.6b)

With the previous chorus celebrating a specific event and ushering the King of glory through the door and a recitative marking the "day," this chorus of perpetual praise stands outside of time, giving us pause for reflection. This crisp chorus is also a contrast to "Lift up your heads" in that it is half the former's length, and employs a double fugue, or a fugue with two subjects, permitting delightful development and contrapuntal activity—the simultaneous unfolding of multiple lines of melody. Looking ahead, this chorus is in the same key as the celebrated "Hallelujah" chorus and employs a similar form, certainly not by accident, as both are hymns of everlasting praise.[34] The voices here are combined in creative ways, with slow voices set atop faster ones, only coming together for the final "him."

36. Countertenor aria

> *Thou art gone up on high, thou hast led captivity captive[,]*
> *and received gifts for men; Yea, even for thine enemies, that*
> *the Lord God might dwell among them. (Psalms 68.18)*

Nos. 36–39 comprise Whitsun, the gift of tongues, and the beginning of evangelism (Part Two, (V)). This strange aria, composed in A–B–A–B form, speaks to the spreading of the Gospel "that the Lord God might dwell among them." The aria feels abstract and distant—even informational in tone when compared with the other, more emotional arias of *Messiah*. Detachment aside, we can appreciate this aria for its elegant construction and ceremonial *coloratura*. The

---

34 Compare the bass entrance "Let all the angels of God" (in No. 35) with the bass entrance for "And he shall reign for ever and ever" (in No. 44).

A–section runs from the beginning through the text "thine enemies" and is marked by leaping intervals, notably "up on high" which is painted first in a gradual ascent and then with a leap to "on" and chromatic descent to "high," as if the countertenor had just made the jump over a precipice and fallen back slightly. The word "receivèd" receives formal *coloratura*, operatic in nature, which lends (more) weight to the aria's tone. The B–section ("that the Lord God might dwell among them") is a contrast for its tranquil demeanor and striking for the painting of "dwell," which is given extensive sequencing and *coloratura* for certain appearances, allowing us to visualize God dwelling as His presence fills the space. The A–B is repeated with variations in the coloratura for "receivèd" and "dwell" and is wrapped in a coda *ritornello* in the strings that pervades the piece throughout and mirrors the introduction.

37. Chorus

The Lord gave the word: Great was the company of the preachers. (Psalms 68.11)

In this chorus, we can hear God's messengers spreading the Gospel far and wide. Handel achieves this effect through the contrast and stacking of three musical motives: First, the opening fanfare, delivered deliberately ("The Lord gave the word"); second, the rhythmic "Great was the company of the preachers"; third, the climbing sixteenth-note setting of "company," first heard in the basses early in the setting. The stacking of "company" in different voices expanding ever higher and in different directions evokes imagery of fellowship and news in excited transit.

38. Countertenor aria

How beautiful are the feet of them that preach the gospel of peace, and bring glad tidings of good things. (Romans 10.15)

In a commendable contrast, Handel counters the frenetic energy of the previous chorus spreading the Gospel to a more soothing focus on the benevolence of those messengers. The setting is a pastoral one,[35] set in a gently rocking four (12/8), with strings framing the opening and closing of the aria. In between, the countertenor sings an easy lullaby, but one with a touch of variation: notice the countertenor's occasional repetition of "how beautiful." Handel devotes the most real estate to "glad tidings," where he gently hints at a major key, before returning to minor. The aria's very existence within a minor key is surprising given its contentment; it succeeds by virtue of the *basso continuo*, which cradles the countertenor with major thirds where needed to strategically sweeten the tone and provide minor-key respite. The text "gospel of peace," for example, receives unexpected major-key treatment from a heretofore menacing bass line that lightens the (counter)tenor of the aria.

39. Chorus

Their sound is gone out into all lands, and their words unto the ends of the world. (Romans 10.18, Psalms 19.4)

To start this chorus, all four voices sing the text "Their sound is gone out" in a delayed and rotating pattern, giving Handel a simple yet effective renewable choral echo effect which paints the scene of the word traveling far and wide. The

---

35 Cf. No. 13.

second motive, "unto the ends of the world," flows effort-lessly from the first, and is set as an ascending and descend-ing scale, beginning with the tenor and followed by soprano, bass, then alto. The voices regroup in unison for "ends of the world" as though they have completed the journey from one end of the globe to the other. Throughout this chorus, Handel sets the text for the voices so that the music is given a pul-sated feel, occasionally with the help of on-the-beat accents from strings, but more often without their help, as Handel sees to it that the voices peak on the beat, thereby ingraining the pulse in the listener with no need of percussion.

40. Bass aria

Why do the nations so furiously rage together, and why do the people imagine a vain thing? The kings of the earth rise up, And the rulers take counsel together Against the Lord and against his anointed. (Psalms 2.1–2.2)

Nos. 40–41 comprise the world's rejection of the Gospel (Part Two, (VI)). This celebrated aria is marked by a constant tremolo in the strings the shaking rage of the towering bass soloist, which recalls his earlier recitative from Part One.[36] With such distinguishing expressive characteristics, there is little room (or need) for motives. Handel gives the aria a fine B–section ("The kings of the earth rise up"), which lends variation to an already riveting piece. An examina-tion of the coloratura reveals that special triplet coloratura is given to "rage" and "imagine," which evokes these words; but also "counsel"—mocking earthly men who would meet and rally against the Lord; and "anointed," a word sanctified

---

36 Cf. No. 5.

with coloratura. "Anointed" is, not coincidentally, the word that ends the aria, making "the Lord and his anointed" the final—if not general—focus.

41. Chorus

Let us break their bonds asunder, And cast away their yokes from us. (Psalms 2.3)

Another crowd or mob chorus,[37] the setting here is intentionally ugly. Unlike the stately echo of the chorus for "The sound is gone out," this repetition is violent, gleeful, and reckless. Instead of easing one motive into the other, Handel gives all musical material equal billing, resulting in anarchy. There is no pulse or hierarchy, only a repeated maddening repetition: "Let-us-let-us-let-us-let-us . . ." revealing the crowd's egocentricity. Even the ending of the chorus, "from us," falls on the first and second beats (rather than the more natural third and first): unbalanced until the end.

42. Tenor recitative

He that dwelleth in heaven shall laugh them to scorn: the Lord shall have them in derision. (Psalms 2.4)

Nos. 42–44 comprise God's triumph (Part Two, (VII)). The tenor's recitative provides a sober contrast to the previous chorus's inebriety and launches him, with venom and piety, into his aria.

43. Tenor aria

Thou shalt break them with a rod of iron; Thou shalt dash them in pieces like a potter's vessel. (Psalms 2.9)

---

37 Cf. No. 28.

Under two minutes, this brief aria is as direct and pitiless as anything to be found in *Messiah*. The *ritornello* in the strings is dominant and unforgiving and matches the fury of the tenor's warning to man of the holy beating that awaits him. The violins' *ritornello* is complemented with a scourging motive from the *basso continuo* (imitated by the tenor: "in pieces"). The *coloratura* that occurs on "rod" and "potter's" is not used to beautify or ornament so much as permit the tenor to work up more of a righteous lather.

44. Chorus

> *Hallelujah, for the Lord God Omnipotent reigneth, Hallelujah! (Revelation 19.6b)*
>
> *The Kingdom of this world is become the Kingdom of our Lord, and of his Christ, and he shall reign for ever and ever, Hallelujah! (Revelation 11.15b)*
>
> *King of Kings, and Lord of Lords, and he shall reign for ever and ever, Hallelujah! (Revelation 19.16b)*

The "Hallelujah" chorus, which concludes God's triumph section and Part II of *Messiah*, is one of the most recognized pieces of classical music in the world. It has been decontextualized so frequently and so liberally,[38] however, that it has become an empty vessel for any festivity, a nondescript expression of blanket joy, thanksgiving, or praise as needed. Returning "Hallelujah" to its original context may help us appreciate its subtlety without fear of lessening its appeal.

---

38 "Hallelujah" was recently featured in a television ad (and more recently withdrawn after Christian protest) hawking Charmin bathroom tissue that featured grateful dancing bears who had been searching for just the right toilet paper—in the woods.

"Hallelujah" appears at No. 44 having earned its exaltations: while it is an anthem of rejoicing and praise, it comes also as a reflection following and resolution of an attempted revolt against God. The "Hallelujah" chorus thus bears the onus of convincingly rebalancing and celebrating the relationship between man and God.

Within a balanced framework, Handel weaves simple motives together and in smart juxtaposition, all the while building tension until an elegant yet humble coda that reinforces unity through unison. The motives are continually varied but inexorably linked. The orchestration is grander than any previous movement, with the trumpets making only their second appearance in *Messiah* (the first being the chorus "Glory to God in the highest" (No. 17)), along with timpani, oboes, and the usual cadre of strings and *basso continuo*. The opening "Hallelujah" motive, an *ostinato*, begins not in the chorus, but in the strings, which presages the chorus's melodic line. Next, a theme is introduced in unison voice and strings: "For the Lord God Omnipotent reigneth," which is straightway met by the "Hallelujah" motive, now used as a response. These two motives are combined. Then another theme is plainly introduced, much in the manner of the previous: "The Kingdom of this world is become the Kingdom of our Lord, and of his Christ." With its simplicity and power, no development of this theme is necessary, and Handel moves directly to a fugal treatment of "and he shall reign for ever and ever," the fugal subject punctuated with "for ever" for rhythmic flavoring. Following that, "King of Kings" is sung by the sopranos and altos in unison, to which the tenors and basses reply "for ever and ever, Hallelujah, Hallelujah," reinstating "Hallelujah" as a responsive *ostinato* and adding "for ever and ever" as another layer for contemplation by the listener. "King of Kings" and "and Lord of Lords" moves from the dominant to the root position, and then ever higher through the scale, permitting Handel to build tension. The "And he shall reign" fugue returns briefly and is then joined magnanimously by "King of Kings," which begins the final section, where the choir recalls all the major themes in unison, capped by a drawn out "Hallelujah!"

Part Three

45. Soprano aria

I know that my Redeemer liveth, and that he shall stand at the latter day upon the earth: And though worms destroy this body, yet in my flesh shall I see God. (Job 19.25–26).

For now is Christ risen from the dead, the first fruits of them that sleep. (I Corinthians 15.20)

Nos. 45–46 comprise the promise of eternal life and triumph over Original Sin (Part Three, (I)). With the question of redemption asked and answered, Handel is freed from dramatic tension and can devote the remainder of *Messiah* to praise of God's victory over Death unfettered by the God vs. Man conflict. For this soprano aria, Handel chooses an extremely lean orchestral accompaniment of unison violins and *basso continuo* that nevertheless cushions the soprano in a gentle 3/4 meter. Dotted rhythms arrive early in the strings, indicating the presence of passion and sympathy[39]—here, for the dead. The dotted rhythms in combination with the

---

39 Cf. No. 22

meter and soothing tone suggest a pastoral setting, though the text provides no such imagery. A *ritornello* is introduced early in the strings and is used to break apart the text, allowing the listener space to reflect on text between the sections of the aria. A transcendent moment occurs in the climax of this aria, the final appearance of "For now is Christ risen," with the soprano climbing the scale, shaping Christ's ascent. The soprano gives a slight drop to "the dead," then tapers off for "sleep." The strings give pause before finishing the phrase in a gentle denouement.

46. Chorus

> *Since by man came death, by man came also the resurrection of the dead. For as in Adam all die, even so in Christ shall all be made alive. (I Corinthians 15.21–22)*

A simple but effective schema is used for this chorus. A slow setting for unaccompanied chorus introduces a faster, livelier accompanied section. In this way Handel capitalizes on the text's parallel structure, introducing a morbid concern in the slow section and allaying that fear in the Allegro response. Slow: "Since by man came death . . ." Fast: ". . . by man came also the resurrection of the dead." Slow: "For as in Adam all die . . ." Fast: ". . . even so in Christ shall all be made alive." While the text in the slow section (question) is repeated twice, the text in fast section (response) is repeated four times, making it doubly weighted, stressing the promise of resurrection over the pain of death.

47. Bass recitative

> *Behold, I tell you a mystery; We shall not all sleep, but we shall all be changed, In a moment, in the twinkling of an eye, at the last trumpet. (I Corinthians 15.51–52)*

Nos. 47–48 comprise The Day of Judgment and general Resurrection (Part Three, (II)). The bass prepares his aria with this recitative, which begins at a whisper (to match "I tell you a mystery") and is given a lush strings accompaniment, which imitates the trumpet call to follow.

48. Bass aria

The trumpet shall sound, and the dead shall be raised incorruptible, and we shall be changed. For this corruptble must put on incorruption, and this mortal must put on immortality. (I Corinthians 15.52–53)

The aria's opening trumpet *ritornello* casts the text "The trumpet shall sound" not as a grim call to the Judgment Day but as a glorious hereafter. This crisp trumpet line is distinctly Handelian for its high Baroque phrasing and polished but easy meandering. The bass sings emphatically and joyfully of the raising of the dead, holding the words "sound" and "raised" in long notes the top of his range, as if to wake the dead. Handel, in setting "and we shall be changed," gives special *coloratura* to the word "changed," which begins, in its first appearance, in a minor key and shifts—or "changes"—to a major key. Handel varies the treatment of "change" in its reappearances, using a dotted eighth-note treatment and a rising scale in turns. Nearly halfway through the aria, a shift in tone occurs in a middle section with the setting "For this corruptible must put on incorruption . . ." (text which alludes to a shift from mortality to immortality). The orchestration is pared down to *basso continuo*, better suited to contemplation than the shimmering brilliance that came before. Here Handel lingers on "put on," giving *coloratura* to the act of donning incorruption and immortality. The A–section then returns; this is a *da capo* aria.

49. Alto recitative

Then shall be brought to pass the saying that is written, Death is swallowed up in victory. (I Corinthians 15.54)

Nos. 49–52 comprise Victory over death and sin (Part Three, (III)). The alto's recitative prepares her duet with tenor to follow. It is *secco* recitative, accompanied only with *basso continuo*. The simplicity here is advantageous in preparing the ear for the antique style of "O death, where is thy sting?"

50. Alto and tenor duet

O death, where is thy sting? O grave, where is thy victory? The sting of death is sin, and the strength of sin is the law. (I Corinthians 15.55–56)

This opening of this brief duet, set for two soloists and *basso continuo*, is lovely for its airy madrigal-like quality, which matches the mocking quality of its text: "O death, where is thy sting? O grave, where is thy victory?" The alto and tenor gang up on Death, repeating their rhetorical questions on top of each other. The running bass adds a feeling of lightness. At times, the soloists juxtapose "O grave, O death," showing that the disdain for their subjects renders them interchangeable. The duet sobers slightly in its B–section, as Handel shifts to a minor key for "The sting of death is sin, and the strength of sin is the law." The alternating pattern of singing from the A–section holds here, and is abruptly interrupted by the chorus.

51. Chorus

But thanks be to God, who giveth us the victory through our Lord Jesus Christ. (I Corinthians 15.57)

Strings rejoin the *basso continuo* along with added oboes as the chorus concludes the passage from I Corinthians in a spirit of thanksgiving. Initially, the chorus continues the motives and rhythm of the previous duet, with "thanks to be to God" mirroring "Where is thy sting?" But a more staid (and minor-key) motive is introduced for "who giveth us the victory through our Lord Jesus Christ." These motives and texts are then alternated several times, but it is "who giveth us the victory . . ." which concludes the chorus, this time in a major key.

52. Countertenor aria

If God be for us, who can be against us? Who shall lay anything to the charge of God's elect? It is God that justifieth: Who is he that condemneth? It is Christ that died, yea rather, that is risen again, who is at the right hand of God, who maketh intercession for us. (Romans 8.31, 33–34)

Messiah's final aria is abstract and contemplative, and is distinguished by interplay between the countertenor and the violins, the only accompaniment apart from *basso continuo*. The violin takes a leading role along with the countertenor, and the two trade phrases throughout. There is no textual painting in this aria, with the *coloratura* serving for general coloration and glorification of God. The emphasis in this setting is placed on "who makes intercession for us," stressing God's role in our lives.

53. Chorus

Worthy is the Lamb that was slain, and hath redeemed us to God by his blood, to receive power, and riches, and wisdom, and strength, and honor, and glory, and blessing. (Revelation 5.12, 5.9)

> *Blessing and honour, glory and power be unto Him that*
> *sitteth upon the throne, and unto the Lamb for ever and ever.*
> *(Revelation 5.13)*

Nos. 53 and 54 comprise the Acclamation of the Messiah (Part Three, (IV)). For the opening of this chorus, Handel employs a similar strategy to the chorus for "Since by man came death . . .",[40] with alternating slow ("Worthy is the Lamb . . . by his blood") and fast ("to receive power . . . and blessing") sections. The orchestration is far more lush than the former, with the addition of oboes, trumpets, and timpani to the strings and *basso continuo*. In the middle section ("Blessing and honour, glory and power be unto Him that sitteth upon the throne"), Handel introduces his most free-wheeling fugue of the work, in which the text is divided and set against itself, only to flow into a unison, then a finale gently staggering and repeating the text "for ever and ever . . ."[41] Handel plays with harmonic ambiguity in the final "for ever," ending on the dominant (A major), holding off on a full cadence by returning to the root (D major) until the beginning of the final "Amen" that follows and brings *Messiah* to a close.

54. Chorus

Amen. (Revelation 5.14)

As Handel earned his "Hallelujah" for the climax of Part Two, he earns his "Amen" for the finale of *Messiah*. "Amen," an expression of solemn ratification (as of an expression of faith)

---

40 Cf. No. 46
41 Cf. Mahler's setting of "ewig" ["forever"] that concludes *Das Lied von der Erde* with a similar arc toward infinity.

or hearty approval, is the proper ending to our journey, rather than "Hallelujah," as is the case (and curse) in truncated performances. Handel's is an elegant and simple Amen (perhaps deceptively so). He begins the movement as a fugue but does not follow through, ending instead in canon, or imitation. Our Amen ends on a final dominant seventh chord—which earns Handel a well-deserved dramatic pause—and closes with a full cadence. Here endeth the lesson.

Chapter 6

~~*M*~~essiah *Recordings*

MESSIAH HAS A RICH RECORDING HISTORY that
stretches back to the beginning of recorded music. Today
there are dozens and dozens of albums to choose from
with aesthetics running the gamut from modern instruments to historically informed performance (HIP) on period
instruments, from small chamber performances to brass-
infused casts of, yes, thousands, from painstaking tributes to
Handel's own myriad versions to revised scores that go well
beyond Mozart into the twentieth century.

The earliest known commercial recording was an abridged
version of the tenor aria "Every valley shall be exalted," performed by W. D. McFarland on a Berliner gramophone disc
from 1898. In 1906, the then Gramophone & Typewriter
Limited Company (G&T)[42] attempted to make a complete
recording of *Messiah*, using more than 20 12-inch and 20-inch
sides. This was the first try at recording a complete *Messiah*

---

42 The U.K.-based Gramophone Company was the parent organization for
the "His Master's Voice" label and merged in 1931 to form Electric and Musical
Industries Limited (EMI).

as well as any complete major choral work. Many of these early recordings reflected the aesthetics of the Victorian era,[43] as evidenced by a plodding 1907 recording featuring 60 select singers from the Leeds Festival Chorus and an unnamed orchestra conducted by Herbert Austin Fricker. A 1909 American recording of "Hallelujah" (Victor) featured the Victor Chorus conducted by Walter B. Rogers, employing a John Philip Sousa brass arrangement of the piece, complete with Sousa's band and the celebrated Sousa sound. The singing, if amateurish, is enthusiastic and astonishingly moving.

Improvements to recording technology in the 1920s made it possible to record the assembled masses of Sir Henry Wood's[44] Handel Festival Choir and Orchestra (Koch), which was gathered for the final Crystal Palace Handel Festival (staged every three years from 1859 to 1926), and composed of 500 orchestral players and 3,000 choristers. Strengthened accompaniments for a full Romantic orchestra were included, including contrabassoons and ophicleides (a keyed bugle). Tempos are deliberate, shock and awe is palpable, and the musicians are rarely together.

Following the decline of Victorian bombast, Sir Thomas Beecham, a great interpreter and revitalizer of *Messiah*, made a famous 1927 recording with the BBC Orchestra and Chorus (Pearl) that uses unfortunate accompaniments by Ebenezer Prout, which Prout based on Mozart's minus those he found to be "un-Handelian"; Prout essentially added density and removed color. The recording retains some hint of the Victorian sound but does well to revitalize the tempos

---

43 See Chapter Four: *Messiah* Revisions

44 Sir Henry founded the celebrated London Promenade Concerts, a.k.a. The Proms.

for *Messiah*, which had been drifting toward the lugubrious. The mastery of Danish tenor Aksel Schiøtz (1906–1975) was captured in a 1940 recording of *Messiah* arias (Danacord). A second Beecham recording in 1947 used Mozart and Prout accompaniments and added Beecham's own reorchestrations (HMV), changing Handel's instrumentation and adding color to superb effect. Beecham's third and final famous (and infamous) 1959 recording of *Messiah* with the Royal Philahrmonic Chorus and Orchestra (RCA) uses a modern orchestration by Eugène Goossen with loads of added brass and percussion that is a masterpiece of Handelian historically oblique performance (HOP), with added piccolos, harps, percussion, and brass that provides an exhilarating if contaminated listening experience.

In the mid-1960s a new wave of *Messiah* recordings—conducted by Colin Davis (Philips), Charles Mackerras (EMI) and Robert Shaw (RCA)—arrived with a greater commitment to authentic Baroque performance. This mid-sized *Messiah* sound will be the most recognizable to listeners who are familiar with the work from traditional local concerts. The recordings employ original instrumentation and were revelatory at the time for their authenticity. A 1976 recording by Neville Marriner and The Academy of St. Martin-in-the-Fields (Decca) takes up the "London version" of *Messiah* (1743) prepared by Christopher Hogwood, a meticulous recreation of how the oratorio was presented from 1743 to 1749.

In 1982, a small-scale *Messiah* was recorded for RCA by Richard Westenburg and the American choral group Musica Sacra, using a chorus of 29 voices. Westenburg's was the first digital *Messiah*. That same year, Christopher Hogwood took the 1754 Foundling Hospital and Covent Garden scores and conducted the Academy of Ancient Music on period instruments accompanied by a boys' choir (Decca). The treble sound of the voices with gut strings and hard timpani mallets make for a tactile listening experience. Among the vocal soloists for this recording is the English soprano Emma Kirkby, whose pure voice, spare use of vibrato and agile coloratura serves as a model for many Baroque specialists. Hogwood's achievement, which is one of the best recordings of *Messiah* on record, ushered in a golden age for *Messiah* recordings, paving the way for recordings by early-music specialists John Eliot Gardiner (Philips), notable for the excellence among the solo singers and its quick tempos; Harry Christophers (Hyperion), who heads The Sixteen in an intimate performance that employs the organ as its keyboard continuo; and Andrew Parrott (Virgin). The latter two recordings feature Kirkby as soprano soloist. A 1984 concert at the Maryland Handel Festival (Intersound Pro Arte) sought to divine the spirit of the 1784 Westminster Abbey commemoration of *Messiah*. Recorded in Washington, DC's National Cathedral, the warm acoustics are certainly comparable with the Abbey's, and this performance with The Smithsonian Concerto Grosso, a hundred-piece period-instrument ensemble, was the largest of its kind assembled since 1784—though it is less than half the size of the 1784 Abbey orchestra. In the late 1980s, Trevor Pinnock struck gold on Archiv, leading the English Concert from the harpsichord; the ensemble played period instruments with a fine roster of soloists, including soprano Arleen Auger, mezzo-soprano Anne Sofie von Otter, countertenor Michael Chance, tenor Howard Crook, and bass John Tomlinson. Of the Mozart *Messiahs* available on disc, Charles Mackerras's (Deutsche Grammophon Archiv) is preferred for its fine soloists and strong chorus work.

The 1990s saw another round of commendable early-music maestros: Martin Pearlman (Telarc), Nicholas McGegan (Harmonia Mundi), Harry Christophers (Hyperion), and Masaaki Suzuki (BIS). The winners of the bunch are the spontaneous yet elegant recording with William Christie with Les Arts Florisants (Harmonia Mundi), which achieves light textures and fresh soloing, and Paul McCreesh's 1997 Gabrieli Consort recording (Archiv), now available on SACD and featuring contralto Bernarda Fink and tenor Charles Daniels. Masaaki Suzuki and the Bach Collegium Japan finds transparency and drama in a 1997 recording (BIS) with fast tempos that do not overreach. In 2004, Cantaloupe Music released "Messiah Remix," featuring digital *Messiah* fantasies and soundscapes by electronic artists and such computer-music composers as Paul Lansky. If the recording is a mixed bag, it speaks to the genius of Handel in proving the malleability of *Messiah* well beyond such pedestrian matters of orchestration, soloists, and tempos.

My personal favorite *Messiah* recording, a faithful companion through the 40 or so listens that I gave the work in aid of the analysis section of this book, is René Jacobs conducting the 1750 version with Freiburg Baroque Orchestra and Choir of Clare College (Harmonia Mundi). Jacobs and his chamber-sized period-instrument ensemble fill *Messiah* with dramatic urgency within a lean framework. The soloists are expressive and imbue their arias with tasteful ornamentation, with countertenor Lawrence Zazzo providing some exotic color.

Conclusion

WHILE THE LUSTER OF POPULAR MUSIC FADES with subsequent hearings, a masterwork only gains in brilliance. Yet a masterwork achieves its greatness not through rote repetition but because of a richness of craft and substance that permits it to be viewed from so many angles that a fresh interpretation is always within the realm of possibility. After over 250 years of continuous performance, having bent to and having survived every conceivable and inconceivable manner of orchestration, having accommodated choirs of a dozen to choirs of thousands (if one includes the public sing-along performances at Christmas), Handel's *Messiah* thrives as ever.

Has the popularity of *Messiah* benefited as a result of its shift from Lenten entertainment to an entrenched Yuletide tradition? Certainly, just as stagings of Charles Dickens' *A Christmas Carol*,[45] the television special "A Charlie Brown

---

45 In an 1844 review of *A Christmas Carol*, the English poet Thomas Hood wrote: "If Christmas, with its ancient and hospitable customs, its social and chari-table observances, were in danger of decay, this is the book that would give them a new lease."

Christmas,"⁴⁶ and The Pogues' ballad "Fairytale of New York" have profited from their Christmastime associations. But, like *Messiah*, all these works transcend the trappings of their season and are masterpieces on their own merits, regardless of context. Is *Messiah* a work of Christian propaganda? Certainly, but to label *Messiah* as such and dismiss it ignores the oratorio's reach, which extends beyond a sectarian audience (by design, not by accident) to provide universal spiritual and psychological insight into the human condition.

Listeners of all faiths can be touched by the innocent joy Handel infuses into "Every valley shall be exalted," the wonderment of "For unto us a child is born," the thanksgiving and reconciliation of "Hallelujah." The human urgency behind "Why do the nations so furiously rage together" is too great to be bounded solely in Christian doctrine and the passionate recitative "Thy rebuke hath broken his heart" legitimately speaks to mortal father-son relationships in addition to the divine one that is its subject. "Since by man came death" offers a reflection on mortality as introspective as any Shakespeare tragedy and Handel's closing "Amen" is as comforting and world-righting as anything in the classical canon. Here's to another 250 years.

---

46 "A Charlie Brown Christmas" has been "performed" every year on network television since 1965.

Glossary of Musical Terms

3/4 Simple triple meter. Three beats per measure with the quarter note being the beat; felt: ONE-two-three.

3/8 Simple triple meter. Three beats per measure with the eighth note being the beat; felt: ONE-two-three.

6/8 Compound triple meter. Six beats per measure with the eighth note being the beat; often felt as two beats: ONE-two-three FOUR-five-six.

12/8 Compound quadruple meter. 12 beats per measure with the eighth note being the beat; often felt as four beats: ONE-two-three FOUR-five-six SEVEN-eight-nine TEN-eleven-twelve.

A–B–A Tripartite musical form, also referred to as ternary form. A–B–A is the fundamental musical form in classical music (and many other genres), based on the principle of departure and return, and of thematic contrast then repetition. The 'A' musical material is separated by a contrasting section, 'B'.

accent The prominence given to a note or notes by a perceptible alteration (usually increase) in volume.

accompanied recitative or *recitative accompagnato* Recitative accompanied by orchestra.

Adagio Italian: "at ease"; "leisurely." A slow tempo lying between *Largo* and *Andante*.

Allegro Italian: "merry"; "cheerful"; "lively." A fast tempo, slower than *Presto*. In its noun form, it can refer to a fast movement.

allemande A Baroque instrumental dance and standard movement of the Baroque suite, the *allemande* is a duple-meter dance.

alto The vocal part lying above the tenor. From the 1500s to the 1700s alto parts were sung by men (falsettists, castratos or high tenors) in sacred music; only in secular music were they sung by women.

anthem A choral setting of a religious or moral text in English that is an offshoot of the motet, generally designed for liturgical performance.

aria Italian: "air." A closed lyrical piece almost always for solo voice, either independent or forming part of an opera or other large work; in the 1600s and 1700s the term was also sometimes applied to instrumental music.

arioso A short air in an opera or oratorio.

aural Of or relating to the ear or to the sense of hearing.

ballad opera An English form in which spoken dialogue alternates with songs set to traditional or popular melodies and sung by the actors themselves. The form was made fashionable by the enormous popularity of John Gay's *The Beggar's Opera* (1728) but faded out by the mid–1730s.

Baroque A term used to designate a period or style of European music covering the years between 1600 and 1750.

Baroque suite A suite of pieces consisting of a number of movements, each in the style of a dance and in the same key.

bass The lowest male voice.

bass line A succession of the lowest notes in a passage or composition which support the other parts and indicate the harmonic progression.

basso continuo An instrumental bass line which runs throughout a piece, over which the player improvises or "realizes" a chordal accompaniment.

binary form A musical structure consisting of two mutually dependent sections of roughly equal duration, usually symbolized as AB or A–B.

cadence A sequence of chords that brings an end to a musical phrase, either in the middle or at the end of a composition.

canon A musical form where the melody or tune is imitated by individual parts at regular intervals.

cantata A work for one or more voices with instrumental accompaniment.

castrato A type of high-voiced male singer. These singers were acquired by castrating young boys with promising voices before they reached puberty. The castrato was central to both church music and opera, in countries under Italian influence, throughout the 1600s and 1700s, and disappeared from Vatican church music only by ~1920; it had vanished from opera by 1830. At the height of their popularity, leading castratos were among the most famous and most highly paid musicians in Europe, and their virtuoso singing method had considerable influence on the development of both oratorio and opera.

chorus A group of singers who perform together either in unison or, most often, in parts; a work, or movement in a work, written for performance by such an ensemble.

coda Closing section of a movement.

coloratura Italian: "coloring." Florid figuration or ornamentation, particularly in vocal music.

common time 4/4 time; quadruple meter; felt: ONE-two-three-four.

compound meter A time signature or meter in which each measure is divided into three or more parts, or two uneven parts—as opposed to two even parts (simple meter), e.g., 6/8.

continuo SEE basso continuo.

contrapuntal Composed according to the rules or techniques of counterpoint.

countertenor A male high voice, originally and still most commonly of alto range, though the title can also be used to describe any adult male voice higher than tenor.

counterpoint Two or more melodic lines sounded simultaneously.

da capo Italian: "from the head." An instruction placed at the end of the last section of a piece or movement indicating that there is to be a recapitulation of the whole or part of the first section.

desk In orchestras, larger sections (e.g., violins) may be subdivided by desk (row number, first desk, second desk, etc.), in addition to section: "first violins," "second violins," etc.

dominant In the tonal system, the harmonically stable fifth degree of the major or minor scale, the triad built upon that degree, or the key that has this triad as its tonic. The dominant chord is an essential part of the full cadence (V–I) in tonal music.

dotted rhythm Rhythms in which notes of longer duration alternate with notes of shorter duration, so-called because the longer notes are usually written with the aid of the dot of addition.

double choir Choir arranged in two equal and complete bodies with a view not merely to singing in eight parts but also to responsive effects.

double fugue A fugue on two subjects.

eighth note A note that is half the value of a quarter note, or one-eighth of a whole note.

figure SEE motive.

French overture A musical introduction for an opera, ballet, or suite that combines a slow opening, marked by stately dotted rhythms, with a lively fugal second section.

fugal subject The defining motive of a fugue.

fugue A compositional technique and musical genre that employs repeated thematic material and imitative counterpoint to explore its subject, usually scored for three to six voices.

gigue A Baroque dance and standard movement in the Baroque Suite, usually in compound meter (e.g., 6/8).

harmonic tension Dissonance in harmony caused by "instable" tones that seek to resolve to "stable" tones.

high Baroque A term used to designate a period or style of European music covering the years between 1700 and 1750.

HIP Historically Informed Performance. A movement by musicians and scholars to approach, research, and perform works of classical music in ways similar to how they may have been performed when they were originally written.

HOP Historically Oblique Performance. Margo Schulter's term for misdirected HIP, a journey to a parallel universe of *Musicologia ficta*.

interval The distance between two notes.

Larghetto A tempo mark indicating a light-hearted *Largo*.

Largo Italian: "large, broad"; a tempo

lauda Italian: "praise"; pl. *laude*. The principal genre of non-liturgical religious song in Italy during the late Middle Ages and Renaissance.

libretto Italian: "small book". A printed or manuscript book giving the literary text, both sung and spoken, of an opera (or other musical work); also the text itself.

madrigal A poetic and musical form created in Italy in the 1300s; also a term used for settings of secular verse in the 1600s and 1700s. During the Baroque period, the madrigal was influential in evolving an expressive relationship between text and music.

major key One of the two modes of the tonal system. Music written in major keys has a positive, affirming character.

masque A genre of entertainment that developed in England during the 1500s and 1600s based around a masked dance.

meter A concept related to an underlying division of time, grouping beats into a recurring pattern. Meter breaks a musical line into stressed and unstressed beats as indicated by a time signature.

minor key One of the two modes of the tonal system. The minor mode can be identified by its dark, melancholic mood.

monody adj. *monodic.* Music consisting of a single line.

motet A form of polyphonic music that reigned from ~1200 to ~1750, shifting in character from sacred to secular and back again over its history.

motive A short musical idea which may take on any or a combination of melodic, harmonic, or rhythmic characteristics. A motive may be of any size, and is most commonly regarded as the shortest subdivision of a theme or phrase that still maintains its identity as an idea. It is most often thought of in melodic terms.

obbligato Italian: "necessary". An adjective or noun referring to an essential instrumental part. The term is often used for a part ranking in importance just below the principal melody and not to be omitted.

opera from Latin *opera,* plural of *opus,* "work"; A drama in which the actors sing throughout.

opera buffa Italian: "comic opera"; a term first applied to the genre of comic opera as it rose to popularity in Italy during the 1700s.

opera seria Italian: "serious opera"; A term used to signify Italian opera of the eighteenth and nineteenth centuries on a heroic or tragic subject.

oratorio An extended cantata of a sacred text made up of dramatic, narrative, and contemplative elements.

oratorio latino An oratorio that employs a text in Latin.

oratorio Passion A Lutheran oratorio form that reached its height in the early 1700s with Bach's *St. John Passion* and *St. Matthew Passion*.

oratorio volgare An oratorio that employs a text in Italian.

ostinato Italian: "obstinate"; the repetition of a musical pattern many times in succession while other musical elements are generally changing.

overture A piece of music of moderate length, either introducing a dramatic work or intended for concert performance.

parlando Italian: "speaking"; a term that denotes a style of singing akin to speech with diminished vocalization.

passacaglia A through-composed variation form constructed over formal harmonic progressions, normally I–IV–V–I, used widely in the Baroque era but with origins in the Spanish street dance, the pasacalle.

passepied A French court dance and instrumental form in use during the 1600s and 1700s; a faster version of the minuet, usually written in 3/8 or 6/8.

Passion The story of the Crucifixion as recorded in the Gospels of Matthew, Mark, Luke, and John. Polyphonic settings of its texts have been made since the 1400s.

pasticcio Italian: "jumble," "hodgepodge," "pudding"; an opera made up of various pieces from different composers or sources and adapted to a new or existing libretto.

pastiche French: "imitation," "parody"; a literary, artistic, musical, or architectural work that imitates the style of a work from another period.

pastoral A literary, dramatic, or musical genre that depicts the characters and scenes of rural life or is expressive of its atmosphere.

pedal point A long, sustained note held through many bars while movement continues in other parts of the piece. The expression is derived from organ playing, where the technique makes use of the organist's ability to hold down a low pedal note indefinitely while playing above it with the hands. The term generally refers to a low bass note, but may also be applied to a long-held note elsewhere in the texture.

polyphony Music in more than one part with the parts moving independently but in harmony.

recapitulation A musical reprise in which opening thematic material returns in a work's finale.

recitative A type of vocal writing, normally for a single voice, with the intent of mimicking dramatic speech in song.

recitativo accompagnato SEE accompanied recitative.

recitativo secco SEE secco recitative.

ripieno Italian: "filled"; denotes the tutti in Baroque orchestral music, distinct from the solo group.

ritornello Italian: diminutive of *ritorno*, or "return"; a short recurring passage that unifies an instrumental or vocal work.

root The lowest note of a vertical sonority or chord.

secco recitative or *recitativo secco* is "dry" recitative—recitative accompanied only by continuo.

senza ripieni A direction requiring all players except those at the leading desks not to play.

sequence A melodic or polyphonic idea consisting of a short figure or motive stated successively at different pitch levels, so that it moves up or down a scale by equidistant intervals.

serenata Italian: from *sereno*, "clear night sky"; a dramatic cantata, normally celebratory or eulogistic, for two or more singers with orchestra. The name alludes to the fact that performance often took place outdoors at night (by artificial light).

setting SEE text-setting.

Siciliana An aria type and instrumental movement normally in a slow 6/8 or 12/8, characterized by clear one- or two-bar phrases with an iambic feeling to the rhythm, simple melodies and clear, direct harmonies; often associated with pastoral scenes and melancholic emotion.

sinfonia Name given in Baroque period to an orchestral piece serving as a three-movement introduction to opera, suite, or cantata.

skipping rhythm SEE dotted rhythm.

sixteenth note A note that is half the value of an eighth note, or one sixteenth of a whole note.

soprano The highest musical range. In vocal music, where it is most common, *soprano* refers directly to the singer: with female voices, it is frequently modified to describe the specific type of voice, such as *lyric soprano* or *dramatic soprano*; it is also used for a boy's treble voice (*boy soprano*) and in the 1600s and 1700s was used for the adult male *castrato* with a high range.

strophic A term applied to songs in which all stanzas of the text are sung to the same music, in contrast to those that are through-composed and have new music for each stanza [SEE *through-composed*].

syncopation The regular shifting of each beat in a measured pattern by the same amount ahead of or behind its normal position in that pattern.

tenor From Latin *tenere*, "to hold"; in polyphony from 1250–1500, the structurally fundamental (or "holding") voice, vocal or instrumental; by the 1400s, *tenor* came to signify the male voice that sang such parts.

text-setting The composition of vocal music to a given text.

theme The musical material on which part or all of a work is based, usually having a recognizable melody and sometimes perceivable as a complete musical expression in itself, independent of the work to which it belongs.

through-composed Written out rather than improvised. The term also describes a composition with a relatively uninterrupted continuity of musical thought and invention. It is particularly applied in contexts where a more sectionalized structure might be expected [SEE *strophic*].

triplet Three notes played in the same amount of time as one or two beats.

Appendix: Messiah Structure

Handel's *Messiah* (1750 version)

Part One

(I) The prophecy of Salvation: the Gospel, "good news"

(II) **The judgment that will accompany the appearance of the Savior**

(III) **The prophecy of the Virgin Birth**

Part Three

Select Bibliography

Bullard, Roger A. *Messiah: The Gospel According to Handel's Oratorio.* Grand Rapids, Michigan: William B. Eerdmans Publishing Company, 1993.

Burrows, Donald. *Handel: Messiah.* New York: Cambridge University Press, 1991.

— Donald. *Master Musicians: Handel.* New York: Oxford University Press, 1994.

Finane, Ben. "Masters Interpret a Master Work", *Newark Star-Ledger.* December 21, 2007.

Handel, George Frideric, Clifford Bartlett, editor. *Messiah* full score. New York: Oxford University Press, 1998.

Hicks, Anthony. "Handel, George Frideric," *Grove Music Online* ed. L. Macy (Accessed 2008). <http://www.grovemusic.com>

Larsen, Jens Peter. *Handel's Messiah.* New York: Norton & Company, second edition, 1972.

Levine, Robert. "Composer: Handel", *Listen: Life With Classical Music.* March–April 2009.

Luckett, Richard. *Handel's Messiah: A Celebration.* London: Harcourt Brace & Company, 1992.

Shaw, Watkins. *A Textual and Historical Companion to Handel's Messiah.* London: Novello & Company Limited, 1965.

— *The Story of Handel's Messiah*. London: Novello & Company Limited, 1963.

Smither, Howard E. *A History of the Oratorio Volume 2: The Oratorio in the Baroque Era Protestant Germany and England*. Chapel Hill: The University of North Carolina Press, 1977.

— *History of the Oratorio Volume 4: The Oratorio in the Nineteenth and Twentieth Centuries*. Chapel Hill: The University of North Carolina Press, 2000.

Steinberg, Michael. *Choral Masterworks: A Listener's Guide*. New York: Oxford University Press, 2005.

Tobin, John. *Handel's Messiah: A Critical Account of the Manuscript Scores and Printed Editions*. New York: St Martin's Press, 1969.

Towe, Teri Noel. "Handel: Messiah," *Choral Music on Record* ed. Alan Blythe. Cambridge: Cambridge University Press, 1991.

Young, Percy M. *Masters of Music: Handel*. New York: David White Company, 1965.

Zondervan, Kenneth Barker, editor. *The Zondervan King James Version Study Bible*. Grand Rapids, Michigan: Zondervan, 2002.

www.ingramcontent.com/pod-product-compliance
Ingram Content Group UK Ltd.
Pitfield, Milton Keynes, MK11 3LW, UK
UKHW020714280225
455688UK00012B/362

9 780826 429438